Parenting in the
Mission of God

Parenting in the Mission of God

AN UPDATED AND EXPANDED EDITION OF
J.C. RYLE'S **THE DUTIES OF PARENTS**

J.C. RYLE
JUSTIN BUCHANAN

SAINTS + SINNERS

Parenting in the Mission of God:
A Revised and Expanded Edition of J.C. Ryle's The Duties of Parents
By J. C. Ryle and Justin Buchanan
Copyright © 2019 by Justin Buchanan

Published by Saints + Sinners
www.saintssinners.net
Saints + Sinners is a ministry devoted to equipping saints and reaching sinners to live in a relationship of worship and obedience to Jesus Christ the King.

Original publication of *The Duties of Parents*
By J. C. (John Charles) Ryle of Liverpool (1816-1900)
Copyright expired. First printed by Wm. Hunt & Co., 1888.

Editor: Lynsey Barry
Cover Designer: Janel Springer | behance.net/janelspringer

ISBN: 978-1-7345227-0-9

To my wife, Sarah:

You make me

a better man,

a better husband,

and a better father.

CONTENTS

PREFACE

John Charles Ryle possessed no aspiration for vocational ministry. He writes, "I never had any particular desire to become a clergyman, and those who fancied that my self will and natural tastes were gratified by it were totally and entirely mistaken. I became a clergyman because I felt shut up to do it, and saw no other course of life open to me."[1]

Ryle was born at Macclesfield in Cheshire County, England on May 10, 1816. His parents were nominal members of the Church of England. Neither his mother nor his father possessed a radical and passionate faith in Jesus Christ. As is often the case, their example became his practice until he was a young man. Ryle describes that time of his life, saying, "I had no true religion at all. . . . I certainly never said my prayers, or read a word of my Bible, from the time I was 7 to the time I was 21."[2] Instead, Ryle attended Eton College and then Oxford where he pursued studies to prepare him for a life of politics and serving in parliament. He also became a standout athlete in rowing and cricket. But a life of politics and parliament would

---

[1] J. C. Ryle, *J. C. Ryle: A Self-Portrait, A Partial Autobiography* (Peter Toon, ed,; Swengel, PA: Reiner Publications, 1975), 59.

[2] Ibid., 35.

never come to fruition for him. God brought him to faith in Jesus Christ and redirected his life for God's glory and purpose.

During his final year at the university, God used three things to awaken Ryle to his need for salvation and a relationship with God. For the first time in many years, he began to read the Bible and pray after he became seriously ill.[3] About this same time, a new church began in Macclesfield where the good news of Jesus' death and resurrection was proclaimed. Up until this time, Ryle noted that "no ministry of the gospel" had been present in any church of that area.[4] He attended the services to hear the evangelical preachers, who clearly and passionately proclaimed the gospel. Additionally, he began to read the writings of evangelical authors including William Wilberforce, Joseph Milner, and John Newton. He read in their works of the transforming power of God's grace through Jesus Christ in their lives, which made an indelible mark upon Ryle's mind, heart, and life.

The work of God culminated one Sunday morning as Ryle attended church. That morning, the rector read from Ephesians. As Ryle heard the Scripture, he was pierced to the heart over his sin and disobedience. He realized how his sin had brought spiritual death and alienation from God in his life. When the rector read the words of Ephesians 2:8–9 that say, "For by grace you have been saved through faith. And this is not your own

---

[3] Ibid., 12.
[4] Ibid., 36.

doing; it is the gift of God," Ryle came to understand that salvation comes by grace alone through faith alone in Christ alone. In that moment, Ryle believed in Jesus Christ and began the journey of following Him. For the rest of his life, he never let go of the words of Ephesians 2:8. Ben Rogers states, "It became the theme of his ministry. It was so central to his life and work that he had it inscribed on his gravestone. You can see it today in the churchyard of All Saints, Childwall, in Liverpool."[5]

Even though Ryle had come to faith in Jesus Christ, his ambition remained to enter politics and join parliament. Once again, God intervened. Through difficult circumstances in his life, Ryle was directed to the work God had laid out for him. Within a few years of his conversion, Ryle's father faced bankruptcy. One of the many consequences of his father's financial failure was that there was no longer any means for him to pursue a life of politics. This season was so traumatic that Ryle later expressed that, had he not been a Christian, he believed he likely would have committed suicide.[6] The difficult circumstance that "ruined" his life came to be regarded later by him as the work of the sovereign hand of God in setting him in the direction he was to go. In that season of despair and

---

[5] Ben Rogers, "Why every seminary student should read J. C. Ryle," *Southern Equip*, accessed June 18, 2019, http://equip.sbts.edu/article/why-every-seminary-student-should-read-j-c-ryle/.

[6] Ryle, *J.C. Ryle: A Self-Portrait*, 54.

desperation, he first entered ministry as a curate in Exbury. His parents expressed great disapproval of his decision. Ryle, however, reflected upon that time saying he sensed no other way he could go. Such was the beginning of his service to Christ, both rural and urban, that constituted a life of ministry spanning 56 years.[7]

Ryle would marry three times, though his first two wives died young. From his second and third marriages, Ryle had one daughter and three sons, respectively. As a husband, father, and shepherd of a local church, he believed in the importance of the family. He held a firm conviction on the primacy of parents to bring up their children to trust in the gospel of Jesus Christ and live as His disciples. His focus on the role of parents may have stemmed from the delinquency of his own parents to lead their children to follow Jesus Christ in a lifetime of faith. But for sure, the writings of the Puritans influenced Ryle's convictions on the role of parents. Their strong teaching that urged parents to accept and excel at their chief duty of leading their children to be Christ's disciples marked Ryle's own thinking, convictions, and practice.[8] Therefore, as a pastor, he aimed to call and teach parents to fulfill the task of making disciples of

---

[7] John Piper, "'The Frank and Manly Mr. Ryle'—The Value of a Masculine Ministry," *Desiring God,* January 31, 2012, accessed June 18, 2019, https://www.desiringgod.org/messages/the-frank-and-manly-mr-ryle-the-value-of-a-masculine-ministry#fn18.

[8] See Iain Murray, *Prepared to Stand Alone* (Carlisle, PA: Banner of Truth Trust, 2016). Murray notes well of Ryle's affinity for the writings of the Puritans.

their children. As a father, he sought to take up this mantle of responsibility in regard to his own children.

The overflow of his desire to shepherd parents in fulfilling the mission of God with their own children was evidenced in Ryle's preaching, as well as his writing. In the year 1860, Ryle's book *The Duties of Parents* was first published to provide practical instruction to parents in how to lead in the spiritual formation of their children. As any reader will note, his words are a timeless treasure. His words are so rooted in the eternal Word of God that they remain as applicable today as they were in the day he first wrote and published them. His original work has been updated and republished through the years to preserve his wise scriptural and practical insights.

This publication, in like manner, preserves the richness of his writing for today's parents. Minimal edits of punctuation or spelling have been made, while the overall message of the original text has been maintained. A significant, distinguishing mark of this volume in contrast to other reprints is the new chapters that form part one. These chapters expand upon the original work of Ryle in order to lay a biblical foundation concerning the God-given role and responsibility of parents as outlined in Scripture. Ryle's original text follows in part two of this book.

As you read, may this work encourage your soul and strengthen your hands for the good work of leading your children, grandchildren, and the next generation to be disciples of Jesus Christ. May we see a generation of children raised up and sent out for the glory of Christ the King, who alone reigns both now and forever.

Justin Buchanan
Edgecliff Village, Texas
August 27, 2019

CHAPTER 1

THE CHIEF PURPOSE OF HUMANITY

Standing on the Palm Beach sandbar in the Curaray River of Ecuador, Jim Elliot and four other men excitedly awaited the arrival of Huaorani Indians. They had observed from the air a group of the Indians moving toward the beach. The beach had been a place where the men previously made contact with a few members of the tribe who were known for their savagery.[1] Jim and the other men did not see the Huaorani for their savagery. Instead, they saw them as a people who had never heard the good news that Jesus died and rose again to redeem them into relationship with God.

Bringing the gospel to the Huaorani of Ecuador had been the motivation for their coming to serve as missionaries. Yet that day in January of 1956 was not to be the day the Indians heard and believed the gospel. Quite to the contrary, the group

---

[1] Tim Chester, "Jim Elliot Was No Fool," *Crossway*, January 8, 2018, accessed May 30, 2019, https://www.crossway.org/articles/jim-elliot-was-no-fool/; Justin Taylor, "They Were No Fools: The Martyrdom of Jim Elliot and Four Other Missionaries," *The Gospel Coalition*, January 8, 2016, accessed May 31, 2019, https://www.thegospelcoalition.org/ blogs/justin-taylor/they-were-no-fools-60-years-ago-today-the-martyrdom-of-jim-elliot-and-four-other-missionaries/.

moving toward the beach ambushed the five missionaries and speared them to death. To the world, and perhaps a number of Christians, the death of Jim and the others was counted a tragic waste.[2] Jim was not yet thirty years of age at the time of his death. He was both a husband and a father. Even so, Jim stood on the beach that day not by accident. He was there as a result of his parents' intentional effort to teach him, even from an early age, that he had been created for a relationship of worship and obedience to God. In that relationship with God, Jim was taught that he was to worship and obey God no matter the cost or consequence.

Growing up in Portland, Oregon, Jim gathered with his family each morning as his father and mother led their family in Bible reading and prayer.[3] In these times of family worship, he learned the supremacy of Scripture, developing a firm conviction that the Bible is necessary and sufficient to direct one's whole life.[4] He not only heard this in his parents' words spoken, but he noted this in their manner of living. In both word and action, Jim's parents stressed the importance of a personal relationship with Jesus Christ. They admonished him from an early age to trust in Jesus Christ and surrender His life for

---

[2] Elisabeth Elliot, *Through Gates of Splendor* (Wheaton, IL: Tyndale House Publishers, Inc., 1996), 247.

[3] Susan Martins Miller, *Jim Elliot: Missionary Martyr* (Uhrichsville, OH: Barbour Publishing, Inc., 1996), 17.

[4] Elliot, *Through Gates of Splendor*, 4.

God's glory and purpose. As a result of their faithful witness, Jim surrendered his life to follow Jesus.

Jim's decision to follow Jesus Christ led him to a radically reoriented life of "single-mindedness and seriousness about spiritual things."[5] He pursued the life his parents taught him he was made for—a life of worship and obedience to God. Enraptured with the glory of God, Jim desired to live a life of worship to God and to lead others to do the same. He wrote in his journal,

> O Jesus, Master and Center and End of all, how long before that Glory is thine which has so long waited Thee? Now there is no thought of Thee among men; then there shall be thought for nothing else. Now other men are praised; then none shall care for any other's merits. Hasten, hasten, Glory of Heaven, take Thy crown, subdue Thy Kingdom, enthrall Thy creatures."[6]

Jim's own worship of God cultivated in him a passion for others to know and worship God. This desire led him to deep contemplation over what God would have for his life. Convinced that God was leading him to take the gospel to those who had never heard, Jim set his sights on the Huaorani in Ecuador. Jim wrote that "[his] going to Ecuador [was] God's counsel" to "a heart which [desired] God."[7] Worshipping and obeying God no matter what God asked was what led Jim to Ecuador, to the Huaorani, to that sandbar, and, ultimately, to die

---

[5] Miller, *Jim Elliot,* 18.
[6] Elliot, *Through Gates of Splendor,* 251.
[7] Ibid, 2.

at the end of a spear. For Jim, his death that fateful day in January 1956 was an offering of worship and obedience to Jesus Christ, his King.

Jim realized the chief purpose of his life was to live in a relationship of worship and obedience to Jesus Christ. He knew this because of his parents' faithfulness to teach and live out this truth. His parents understood the greatest need in their children's lives was for them to return into a relationship with Jesus through faith in Him and His death and resurrection. They grasped that only a relationship with Jesus would enable their children to live again in the relationship for which they were made. They impressed this truth upon their children's hearts and directed them to be transformed by the redeeming power of Christ.

God made humanity to live in a relationship of worship and obedience with Him. Humanity has been made for this relationship, and parents have been entrusted with the chief duty of leading their children into this relationship with God through Jesus. Scripture teaches this truth to us from its beginning pages.

CREATED TO WORSHIP AND OBEY

The Bible begins with a record of God's work to create all things. In this account, Scripture teaches us that God created humanity for a special relationship with Him. The Scripture says that humanity was made as a unique creation, with a unique distinction, for a unique intention.

A UNIQUE CREATION

In the first five days of creation, God spoke into existence celestial bodies, earthly vegetation, sea-life, and the animal kingdom. On the sixth day, however, we observe the final act of His work as He sculpted human beings. God did not create humanity in the same way He created everything else.

The Triune God—Father, Son, and Spirit—counseled together before creating male and female. God says in Genesis 1:26, "Let us make man in our image…" At no other time in the creation account does God stop, take divine counsel, and then act to create. Humanity, however, was not just any other part of creation. Human life came as the pinnacle and crowing achievement of God's work.[8]

Having counseled together, the Trinity acted to create humanity. Everything God created prior to humanity was spoken into existence. Yet when the time came to create man and woman, God chose to form man by His own hands from the dust of the ground and fashion the woman by His own hands from the rib of the man (Gen 2:7, 21–22). All of this highlights that God "created Adam and Eve in a special, personal way."[9]

---

[8] Kenneth Mathews, "Genesis 1-11:26," in *The New American Commentary*, vol. 1A (Nashville, TN: Broadman & Holman Publishers, 1996), 160.

[9] Wayne Grudem, *Systematic Theology* (Grand Rapids, MI: Inter-Varsity

God, the master sculptor, molded the physical frames of both male and female into their divinely chosen shape. He then breathed into their bodies His breath in order to make humanity a living being (Gen 2:7).[10] Human beings are a unique creation of God.

A UNIQUE DISTINCTION

Man and woman's uniqueness among God's creation can be observed beyond the unique act of their creation. We also see God bestow a unique distinction upon man and woman. When God took counsel within the Godhead, He declared that He would create humanity in His own image and likeness (Gen 1:27). Human beings were made to bear the likeness of God upon this earth. No other part of creation can claim to be God's image bearers.

The Apostle Paul wrote in Romans 1 that all creation reveals the invisible attributes of God. His divine nature and eternal power are displayed in His creation. The psalmist stated in Psalm 19 that the heavens declare the glory of God and communicate about Him day and night. All of creation declares the existence and power of God. But all creation does not bear the image or likeness of God. Only humanity holds the unique distinction of bearing the image of God. Being image bearers

Press, 1994), 265.
[10] Victor P. Hamilton, "Genesis," in *Evangelical Commentary on the Bible*, vol. 3, Baker Reference Library (Grand Rapids, MI: Baker Book House, 1995), 12.

means "that humans share, although imperfectly, in the nature of God—that is, they were given the communicable attributes of intelligence, knowledge, spiritual understanding, creativity, wisdom, love, compassion, holiness, justice, and the like."[11] Humans would also bear God's image in that they were made for relationship. David Turner writes, "Just as the Creator is a being in relationship, so are his creatures."[12]

The distinction of being sole image bearers of God brought with it the responsibility for humanity to exercise God's authority over His creation. Man and woman were entrusted with "the responsibility to rule as [God's] vice-regents over the earth."[13] Only human beings are image bearers of God who possess the authority to rule and reign with God over every other part of His created world. Even after humanity's rebellion against God, Scripture declares that human beings still bear the image of God (Gen 5:1–3, 9:6) and possess authority and responsibility in ruling over and caring for God's creation.

---

[11] Allen Ross and John N. Oswalt, *Cornerstone Biblical Commentary: Genesis, Exodus*, vol. 1 (Carol Stream, IL: Tyndale House Publishers, 2008), 39.

[12] David L. Turner, "Image of God," in *Evangelical Dictionary of Biblical Theology*, electronic ed., Baker Reference Library (Grand Rapids: Baker Book House, 1996), 366.

[13] Bruce Waltke and Charles Yu, *An Old Testament Theology* (Grand Rapids, MI: Zondervan, 2007), 218.

A UNIQUE INTENTION

Uniquely created in the image of God to exercise His authority over creation, humanity was also created with a unique intention. More than just reflecting Him upon the earth or ruling upon the earth, God intended humanity to share in and enjoy a relationship with Him like no other part of creation was made to experience in the same way. God created man and woman and put them into the garden He had constructed for them in Eden (Gen 2:8) to fulfill His intent—their purpose—of living in a relationship of worship and obedience to Him as faithful followers.

MADE TO WORSHIP AND OBEY

We read twice in Genesis 2 that God took the man and woman and *put* them into the garden in Eden. We read in Genesis 2:8, "And the Lord God planted a garden in Eden, in the east, and there he put the man whom he had formed." Then, in Genesis 2:15, Moses says, "The Lord God took the man and put him in the Garden of Eden to work it and keep it." Moses was not merely repeating himself for effect. Rather, he intended to communicate to the reader two critical details in God's work. Moses aimed to tell us *where* God placed humanity to live and then to declare to us *why* God placed humanity to live there. In Genesis 2:8, we learn the *place* where humanity would live— the garden. In Genesis 2:15, we learn the *purpose* for which they were placed to live there—to live in a relationship of worship and obedience to God.

Both verses say God *put* humanity in the garden. Unfortunately, the English does not pick up the fact that the Hebrew word translated *put* is not the same in both verses. The first word Moses used for *put* is a common term that reflects the idea of setting something in place. Thus, this verse states that God set or placed Adam and Eve into their home in the garden. But when Moses penned Genesis 2:15, he did not use the common word for *put*. Instead, he selected a Hebrew word that meant being set apart in God's presence. The word carries the meaning of being designated for special use by God.[14] Humanity was not put in the garden just as his place to live and work. Man and woman were set apart in the garden as an instrument to bring glory to God through their relationship with Him as their Creator and King.

Most English translations of Genesis 2:15 translate the end of the verse to say that God put humanity in the garden to "work it and keep it." Translating this verse in this way seems to suggest that humanity was placed there to work and keep the *garden*. If this is accurate, we could conclude that God put humanity in the garden to primarily *do* something rather than to ultimately *be* something.[15] This translation, however, poorly

---

[14] John Sailhamer, "Genesis," in *The Expositor's Bible Commentary*, ed. Frank Gæbelein, vol. 2 (Grand Rapids, Mich.: Zondervan, 1990), 44–45.

[15] Various commentators assert that the purpose of man's existence in the

reflects the Hebrew text and does not capture the heart of God as to why He made humanity and placed them in the garden.

The words typically translated "work it and keep it" should not be understood as referring to humanity's work of caring for the garden. They refer not to the garden, but to God Himself.[16] Moses used the words to *work* and to *keep* "throughout the Pentateuch for spiritual service."[17] The word *work* means to *serve*. Moses would use this word elsewhere to speak of worship and service to the Lord.[18] The term *keep* is used in the Old Testament to speak of obeying God's Word and keeping His commands. Moses employed both of these words elsewhere in the Old Testament to describe the work of the priests. The priests were to faithfully obey the commands of God in carrying out the prescribed instructions for worship to God in the

---

garden was for the primary task of doing something for God, namely to oversee and cultivate the garden. Kenneth Mathews writes, "God gives the man a purposeful existence that includes overseeing his environment. Work is a God-given assignment and not a cursed condition." See Kenneth Mathews, *Genesis 1-11:26*, vol. 1A, The New American Commentary (Nashville: Broadman & Holman Publishers, 1996), 209. Victor Hamilton asserts, "Work is not a result of the fall; manual labor is prefall. Adam is put into the garden to work it and to take care of it (2:15–17)." See Victor P. Hamilton, "Genesis," in *Evangelical Commentary on the Bible*, vol. 3, Baker Reference Library (Grand Rapids, MI: Baker Book House, 1995), 12.

Walter Brueggermann contends that humanity is "to care for and tend the garden." He says the wording of the text "may suggest a gardener or a shepherd. In either case, work belongs to the garden." Brueggermann concludes that from the beginning God intended humanity to be workers in the garden, primarily. Thus he states, "Work is good, surely, to enhance the garden." See Walter Brueggermann, "Genesis," in *Interpretation: A Bible Commentary* (Louisville, KY: Westminster John Knox Press, 1982), 46.

[16] Sailhamer, "Genesis," 45.

[17] Allen Ross, *Creation & Blessing* (Grand Rapids, MI: Baker Book House Company, 1988), 124.

[18] Ibid.

tabernacle.[19] Moses shows the "relationship between Eden and tabernacle" in order to direct us to see God's purpose for humanity in the garden as ultimately one of worship and obedience to God.[20]

God placed humanity in the garden for the purpose to worship and obey. Thus, the garden was more than a field to be worked; it was a sanctuary for worship. The garden was more than a home in which to exist. The Garden of Eden was hallowed ground where humanity was to live in God's presence, before God's face, in undivided worship and obedience to Him. John Sailhamer affirms this understanding, writing, "Man is put in the garden to worship and obey [God]. Man's life in the garden was to be characterized by worship and obedience; he was a priest, not merely a worker and keeper of the garden."[21]

MADE TO REST IN GOD AND HIS WORK

God placed humanity in the garden for relationship. This relationship was to be enjoyed within the protection and peace of God and by resting in His work. Not only does the word *put* used in Genesis 2:15 mean to be placed in God's presence or

---

[19] Ross and Oswalt, *Cornerstone Biblical Commentary: Genesis, Exodus*, 46.

[20] Scott Aniol, "Man's purpose is to worship and obey," *Religious Affections Ministries*, August 31, 2011, accessed May 15, 2019, https://religiousaffections.org/articles/articles-on-worship/mans-purpose-is-to-worship-and-obey/; Sailhamer, "Genesis," 45; Mathews, "Genesis 1-11:26," 210.

[21] Sailhamer, "Genesis," 45.

designated for special use to God, it also means to be placed in the safety and rest of God.

When God put humanity in the garden, He put them in a place where they could rest in His work and find safety and identity in their intimate relationship with Him. Humanity would not find rest or safety outside of relationship with God and His work. Apart from God, there would be no peace or security. They would not assume a greater identity and purpose apart from their relationship with Him. Their own work would never prove more important to who they were or what they were made to be than God's work. Humanity's peace, identity, and security come from relationship with God and His work—nothing else. For this reason, God established a regulative pattern of rest in humanity's normal routine of life as a prompt to always point us to the necessity of our relationship with God and the necessity of resting in His work.

Man and woman's first day upon the earth was a day commissioned by God for rest. God created humanity on the sixth day of creation and then rested on the seventh. On the first day of humanity's existence on the planet, we were not to work. We were to rest in and reflect upon the work of God. Mankind had done nothing to create the world. We had done nothing to create or earn a relationship with God. Our first day on this planet was set apart for rest so man and woman would be pointed back to God. Only when humanity ceases from his own labor and striving can he focus upon God and His all-sufficient work. The day of rest was to calibrate the human heart to find security, rest, and identity in God's completed work and our relationship with Him.

Throughout the history of God's people in the Old Testament, God continually called His people to remember the Sabbath day as a holy day for worship, not human effort. God continually called His people to remember Him and rest in His work and salvation because one of the tragic consequences of sin is humanity's erroneous trust in his work and achievements. We strive even for the salvation our souls all desperately need. However, in establishing a day of rest, God sought to direct His people away from the work of their hands to the person and work of God (Ex 20:8, Deut 5:12–14). He placed a weekly reminder in our schedule aimed at diverting us away from what we can do for God and directing us to trust in what God has already done for us.

The Sabbath day of rest would find its ultimate fulfillment in the person of Jesus Christ. Jesus is the ultimate rest to the human heart weary with sin and burdened with the inability to atone for our mistakes and (Heb 4:1–11). Jesus' death and resurrection was God's completed and sufficient work to restore our relationship with God that was severed by sin. No amount of striving or labor can gain us salvation. Try as we might to obtain redemption through our own works, all our efforts to earn salvation leave us worn out and weary. We strive in vain to gain salvation through good works because redemption is only received through the completed work of Jesus Christ. By trusting in Him we find rest, safety, and identity. Our peace and security come through relationship with Him. We do not look to a day of physical rest but to the Deliverer of eternal, spiritual rest. Jesus gives rest to the weary soul starving and striving for salvation. Jesus provides true identity as redeemed image bearers. In the beginning, God put humanity in the garden as His image bearers to have rest, peace, and security in relationship with Him and His sufficient work.

MADE TO KEEP GOD'S CREATION

Does all this mean that humanity had no "work" to do in caring for God's creation? Adam and Eve did have a role in maintaining the creation of God. The issue is that we have misunderstood the primary way humanity was to care for God's world. Man and woman would maintain God's creation not by manual labor but through spiritual service. Should humanity cease to live in a relationship of worship and obedience to God, their rebellion would bring ruin upon all God made. God states this clearly in the verse immediately following Genesis 2:15.

God permits mankind to eat of every tree of the garden but one—the tree of the knowledge of good and evil (Gen 2:16–17). He declared that to eat of the tree of the knowledge of good and evil would bring catastrophic destruction upon humanity and the world. An act of disobedience in eating of that tree would result in humanity's broken relationship with God, one another, creation, and oneself.[22] Sin would plunge a perfect world in to chaos and destruction. Thus, Adam and Eve were to "guard" and "keep" God's creation by living in a relationship of worship and obedience with Him.[23] To focus on physical work as the primary means of keeping God's creation misses the scriptural context. The Scripture is clear that humanity would preserve the work of God only through faithful spiritual service to God. When in Genesis 3 humanity failed to worship and obey God, the world God made succumbed to ruin and destruction.

HUMANITY'S FAILURE

A serpent entered the garden to tempt Adam and Eve in Genesis 3. The serpent, Satan, came to tempt humanity to do what he had already done. He who had already rejected God in an effort to take the throne of the Most High God came into the garden to entice humanity to rebel and sin against God (Rev 12:9, 20:2). His effort, however, required the crafting of a compelling lie. Satan's lie twisted the truth rather than outright reject what God had spoken. Satan stated that God had not spoken truthfully to humanity when He told them they would die if they ate of the

---

[22] Francis Schaeffer, *Pollution and the Death of Man: A Christian View of Ecology* (Wheaton, IL: Tyndale House, 1970), 66–68.

[23] William David Reyburn and Euan McG. Fry, *A Handbook on Genesis*, UBS Handbook Series (New York, NY: United Bible Societies, 1998), 69.

tree of the knowledge of good and evil. Satan said that if they ate of the tree they would become their own gods like God. Were they to become their own gods, they would no longer be required to worship and obey God. Being their own gods would allow them to choose for themselves who or what they worshipped, as well as to decide what was either good or evil to be obeyed or disregarded (Gen 3:5). Satan held out before humanity an alternative life where they could replace God or, at the very least, dispose of their need for Him. Satan's temptation and lie took aim at the very heart of the purpose for which man and woman had been created.

Satan led humanity down a path to disbelieve God as pure and trustworthy. He succeeded in his goal. Paul wrote that humanity exchanged the truth of God for the lie. The lie undergirding all other lies and every sin is the lie that the creation can be worshipped and obeyed in place of the Creator (Rom 1:25). Adam and Eve believed this lie and ceased to find their "superior satisfaction" in God. Rather, they longed for the superior satisfaction of being their own god.[24] So they ate of the tree of the knowledge of good and evil in a quest to secure their divine status and authority.

Humanity's outward action of eating the fruit of the tree reflected an inward shift of their heart. Rebellion occurred first

---

[24] John Piper, "Did Adam and Eve Sin Before the Bite?" *Desiring God*, September 18, 2017, accessed May 24, 2019, https://www.desiringgod.org/interviews/did-adam-and-eve-sin-before-the-bite.

inwardly before it demonstrated itself outwardly. Sin occurs when our lust or desire conceives in the heart (Jam 1:15). Only after sin conceives is there an outward manifestation of disobedience (Prov 4:23, Matt 15:11, Luke 6:45). Adam and Eve's act of disobedience in eating of the tree of the knowledge of good and evil merely revealed the state of their rebellious hearts. In their hearts, God had already been disbelieved and dethroned in an effort to "make [themselves] supreme in the little kingdom of Mansoul."[25] John Piper explains,

> When Adam and Eve used their biceps and triceps and hand muscles to reach for the forbidden fruit and then used their jaw muscles to bite it, those outward acts of the muscles were evil precisely because they were expressions of a heart that had lost its taste for the superior satisfaction of God and had become dominated by desires for something more than God.[26]

Eating of the tree of the knowledge of good and evil was the first act of a human race now living as "usurpers" sitting upon a

---

[25] A. W. Tozer, *The Knowledge of the Holy* (San Francisco, CA: HarperSanFrancisco, 1961), 30.

[26] Piper, "Did Adam and Eve Sin Before the Bite?"

John MacArthur agrees with Piper on this point. He notes, "Behavior simply reflects what is in the heart. In Mark 7:21-23, Jesus said, 'From within, out of the heart of men, proceed evil thoughts, adulteries, fornications, murders, thefts, covetousness, wickedness, deceit, lewdness, and evil eye, blasphemy, pride, foolishness. All these evil things come from within and defile a man." He goes on to observe, "Many other biblical passages teach the same thing: bad behavior stems from a corrupt heart." See John MacArthur, *The Fulfilled Family* (Nashville, TN: Nelson Books, 2005), 114–115.

Additionally, John Stott points to the inward sin as being the cause of the outward egregious acts of disobedience. He notes, "The sins we commit are merely outward and visible expressions of this inward and invisible malady. Jesus explained that just as the character of the fruit depends on the character of the tree, so our actions are determined by our hearts." See John Stott, *Basic Christianity* (Chicago, IL: Inter-Varsity Press, 1964), 76.

"stolen throne." [27] Our sin has always been an effort to steal the throne of God whose one and only rightful occupant is Jesus Christ, Son of the Living God. He is the Supreme Ruler to be worshipped and obeyed forever.

Failure to worship and obey God brought ruin to the remarkable creation of God, just as He had declared it would. A. W. Tozer writes, "The whole course of life is upset by failure to put God where He belongs. We exalt ourselves instead of God and the curse follows."[28] Mankind deviated from the intended purpose for which he had been created. Man and woman engaged in a sinister plot to rewrite and recast humanity's God-given purpose. They believed it possible to reshape their purpose from being created image bearers who lived in worship and obedience with Him to being their own gods who were worshipped and obeyed in His place. Today, sinful men and women still desire to be objects of worship and obey. But this was never what God intended.

PARENTING AND THE PURPOSE OF HUMANITY

Understanding that our purpose as human beings is to live in a relationship of worship and obedience to God is critically important to the role and responsibility of parents. Every parent and child has been created to live in relationship to God. This

---

[27] Tozer, *The Knowledge of the Holy*, 30.
[28] A. W. Tozer, *The Pursuit of God* (Camp Hill, PA: WingSpread Publishers, 1993), 100.

truth informs parents and children as to the purpose of their existence, as well as how God meant their lives to be lived here on earth. As a result, this truth brings has significant implications and applications.

The *first* implication is that parents must embrace, first and foremost, that they were made for a relationship of worship and obedience with God. God made fathers and mothers to be, first of all, image bearers of God who live in a relationship with Him. This brings parents to realize the necessity of trusting in Jesus Christ in order to have the relationship with God that sin destroyed. Without this relationship, parents are unable to fulfill their God-given purpose. But when they trust in Jesus Christ, they receive new life and relationship with God. As a result, their life experiences a radical reorientation that leads them to submit all that they are and all that they have, including their children, to God as Creator and King.[29]

A *second* implication is that fathers and mothers see their children as having been created by God for a relationship with God. God's act of blessing parents with children is for the purpose of seeing that those parents return their children to God for a relationship with Him. Children are not about fulfilling parents' dreams or ideals of what their family should be or look like. Children are not the symbols of status or success for parents. They are a gift of God to be stewarded for His glory.

---

[29] Andrew Murray, *Absolute Surrender* (Abbotsford, WI: Aneko Press, 2017), 59.

Our children have been formed by God to fulfill the purpose of living for His glory and praise in a relationship with Him. Parents who understand humanity's God-given purpose for themselves and their children prioritize above all else their children's reconciled relationship to God. This requires parents to embrace, above all competing ideals and earthly goals, the importance of their children knowing God in a personal relationship and growing in Him. The wise parent sets no greater goal or earthly glory before their children than to live wholly devoted to God in worship and obedience.

A *third* implication is that the gospel is indispensable for parents and children to have the relationship for which they were made. The only means by which humanity can have a relationship with God again is through the gospel of Jesus Christ. The next chapter will deal with this more. But here it is important to state briefly the necessity of the gospel to parents and children in fulfilling their God-given purpose. Parents and children are image bearers of God who were made to live in a relationship with Him that has been breached by the disobedience of humanity. We all have inherited, as a result, a sinful nature and have sinned against God. Our sin has alienated us from the life and relationship we were made to enjoy in God. Until the chasm be spanned that sin has produced, no human being can live in the reconciled relationship with God he or she has been made to experience. If a person's relationship with

God is not reconciled, he or she cannot fulfill the purpose for which God has made them.

The gospel declares that there is rescue from our sin and restoration of our relationship with God. Jesus Christ died to pay the penalty for sin and bridge the gap between God and man. Nothing else but the gospel of Jesus Christ will do to correct what humanity's sin corrupted. If parents and their children are ever to enjoy relationship with God, they must "repent and believe the gospel" (Mark 1:15). The gospel, the good news of Christ's sacrifice and resurrection, promises a restored relationship with God to parents, their children, and all who are far from God (Acts 2:39). Faith in Jesus Christ through the gospel is critical to make peace with God for us and bring us back to Him. Parents must place their faith in Jesus and proclaim the gospel to their children. They must project the gospel also in daily life, relationships, and situations. Parents must set the gospel at the center of their lives, their homes, and their parenting. The gospel is indispensable for parents and children to live in relationship with God and fulfill the purpose for which God created us.

FROM CHIEF PURPOSE TO CHIEF MISSION

The chief purpose for both parents and children is to live in a relationship of worship and obedience to the God who loves and created us. Because this is the chief purpose of all people, God's mission from the beginning has been to multiply upon the earth image-bearing followers who live in this kind of relationship to Him. In God's plan for the family and the role and responsibility of parents, God designed parents to be partners with him in this mission.

We will see in the next chapter that because the chief purpose of humanity is to live in a relationship of worship and obedience to God, the chief mission of parents is to lead their children back into community with God. The chief mission of parents is to make disciples of their children.

CHAPTER 2

THE CHIEF MISSION OF PARENTS

Edward returned to England to live luxuriously off the wealth he accumulated as an indigo farmer in India. He moved his family into a large estate in Tidworth, England. He then began pursuing the many passions his wealth allowed him to experience. He enjoyed card playing, watching sports, the theatre, hunting, and horseracing. His son Charles later stated, "My father was just a man of the world, loving all sorts of worldly things. He had made a fortune in India and had come back to England to spend it."[1] Edward's example was not lost on his sons. They took what they saw in his example and lived as though the greatest pursuit in life is for one's own glory, pleasure, and happiness.

A radical change occurred in Edward's life, however, when he and his wife accompanied friends to hear Dwight Moody preach at the Drury Lane Theatre. Though he reluctantly agreed to go, what he heard that evening stirred in him a desire to keep

---

[1] Delavan Leonard Pierson, ed., *Northfield Echoes: Northfield Conference Addresses, Volume 4* (East Northfield, MA: Northfield Echoes, 1897), 262.

coming back night after night. By the end of the week, Edward trusted in Jesus Christ for salvation. This decision turned his life upside down.

Radical changes and realignments took place quickly. He became passionate about God's mission to make disciples. His passion to make disciples led Edward to reevaluate his role and responsibility as a father. Seeing that his greatest mission was making disciples, he realized the greatest disciples he could make were those of his own children. Therefore, he became chiefly concerned with the spiritual state of his sons who were away attending school at Eton College. He determined that he would do all that he could to influence and lead his children to faith in Jesus. So he invited his three sons to meet him in London where he planned to take them to hear Moody preach just as his friend had done with him.

When Edward and his sons met in London, he shared how he had placed his faith in Jesus Christ. He explained how that decision had altered his life. Shocked by their father's admission of becoming a Christian, and speechless at his plan to take them to hear a preacher instead of enjoying some other form of entertainment, the three young men hesitantly agreed to go.

None of the three young men chose to place their faith in Jesus and dedicate their lives to follow Him that evening. Even so, their father continued to seek how he might lead them to follow Jesus. Over the coming weeks and months, God used the continual witness of Edward and his wife in the lives of their sons. While they were home from school the following summer, God used a visiting preacher whom Edward had invited into their home to lead all three to trust in Jesus Christ on the same day.

Reflecting on his decision to devote his life to follow Jesus Christ, Charles pointed to the importance of his father's influence. Most significant for Charles was the change he witnessed in his father's life. He wrote, "...I had the good fortune to meet a real live play-the-game Christian. It was my own father."[2] God rescued Edward from living in pursuit of his own glory and pleasure to living in a relationship of worship and obedience to Jesus Christ. His sons observed the transformation and reorientation of their father's life and they too surrendered their lives by faith to follow Jesus.

Charles Studd, also known as C. T. Studd, gave up popularity and the lucrative life as a sports star in order to be sent as a missionary. His father's passion to proclaim the gospel and make disciples led Charles to carry the gospel to the nations. As a result, he ended up founding the Heart of Africa Mission and gave his life in obedient service to Christ. He once declared, "Some want to live within the sound of a church or chapel bell; I want to run a rescue shop within a yard of hell."[3]

---

[2] Norman Grubb, *C. T. Studd: Athlete and Pioneer* (Atlantic City, N.J.: The World-Wide Revival prayer Movement, 1947), 21.

Charles' journey began when his father embraced his role and responsibility to make disciples of his children. Charles was taught to know, follow, and grow up into Jesus Christ by his parents, especially his father. It is doubtful the world will ever fully know the impact of Charles' life of worship and obedience to God.

A MISSION ENTRUSTED TO PARENTS

The chief mission of every parent is to lead their children to faith as disciples of Jesus Christ. A disciple is a person who lives in a relationship of worship and obedience under Jesus' rule and reign. They have come to recognize the supremacy and glory of Jesus Christ above all else, and they have devoted themselves wholly to Him.[4]

Parents fulfill the mission of making disciples of their children by leading them to know, follow, and grow in Jesus Christ. Making disciples is a parent's greatest mission because it is at the heart of God's mission. In both the Old and New Testaments of the Bible, we understand that God's mission has been always to see all nations return into a relationship of worship and obedience to Him as His followers. In both the Old

---

[3] Bruce Barton, David Veerman, and Neil Wilson, "1 Timothy," *Life Application Bible Commentary* (Wheaton, IL: Tyndale House Publishers, 1993), 36.

[4] See John Piper, *Taste and See* (New York, NY: Multnomah, 2005); Richard Ross, *Student Ministry and the Supremacy of Christ* (Bloomington, IN: CrossBooks, 2009).

and New Testaments, we see as well that God designed to serve a critical, lead role in this mission as it relates to their children.

GOD'S UNCHANGING MISSION

God's mission to make disciples of all nations was not a new idea He unveiled with the incarnation and earthly ministry of Jesus Christ. This mission was not implemented first when Jesus spoke the words of the Great Commission to His disciples following His death and resurrection. Making disciples was not an invention of the Church in the New Testament.

The coming of Jesus Christ was necessary for humanity to live once again in intimate, worshipping, obedient community with God. Only the death and resurrection of Jesus Christ could undo what our sin has done. His death and resurrection provides atonement for sin and restores us into a right relationship of worship and obedience to God again. His atoning work makes possible for us to be the image bearers of Christ we were made to be at creation (Rom 8:29). Jesus' work through His incarnation, death and resurrection are necessary to fulfill God's mission of making disciples. But His coming was not the beginning of this mission. When Jesus instructed His disciples, following His death and resurrection, to proclaim the gospel in all the earth through the power of the Holy Spirit so that others could by faith return as His followers, His command communicated the mission of God that had existed from the beginning (Matt 28:19–20, Mk 16:15, Lk 24:46–49, Jn 20:21, Acts 1:8).

God had already articulated to humanity His mission of making disciples well before Jesus uttered the words of the Great Commission. From the beginning of creation, and before the fall of humanity, God intended humanity as His image bearers to faithfully multiply more image bearers on the earth who lived in worshipping, obedient relationship with Him.

THE GREAT COMMISSION IN GENESIS

The mission of God to multiply image bearers was entrusted to parents in the garden prior to sin fracturing our relationship with God.[5] God enlisted humanity in making disciples as partners with Him. Man and woman would accomplish this through the family God designed. When God brought the man and woman together in relationship, He instituted "marriage, and thereby the family, as the core engine for filling the earth with His people."[6] The family was God's chosen instrument to multiply image-bearing followers of God upon the earth who lived in a relationship of worship and obedience with Him.

The first time Scripture records God speaking to human beings is in Genesis 1:28. Here, God pronounced a blessing on

---

[5] Henry T. Blackaby and Avery Willis, *On Mission with God: Living God's Purpose for God's Glory* (Nashville, TN: Broadman and Holman Publishers, 2002), 253.

[6] Rob Rienow, *Limited Church, Unlimited Kingdom* (Nashville, TN: Randall House, 2013), 148.

the man and woman to bear children (be fruitful) and multiply on the earth. The first husband and wife were instructed to reproduce after their own kind just as God had created plants and animals to reproduce after their kind. Through God's gift of sexual intimacy in the marriage relationship, a husband and wife would conceive and give birth to a child made in the image of God. The child conceived and born was then to be led, by his father and mother, to live as an image bearer of God in a relationship of worship and obedience to Him.[7] God's blessing upon humanity to be fruitful in bearing children was a "function" of responsibility to advance the mission of God.[8] The divine blessing God pronounced over humanity, enabling them to bear fruit and multiply, gave Adam and Eve ability and authority to join with God as co-creators.

THE INTERRUPTION OF THE GREAT COMMISSION

Originally, humanity would fulfill God's mission to make disciples in the garden by having children and teaching them to live in relationship with God. In the perfect garden, children would be born without any interruption or impediment to a relationship with God. Fathers and mothers would welcome into the world their children as image bearers of God who bore no

---

[7] Gordon J. Wenham, "Genesis," in *New Bible Commentary: 21st Century Edition*, ed. D. A. Carson et al., 4th ed. (Downers Grove, IL: Inter-Varsity Press, 1994), 61.

[8] Derek Kidner, *Genesis: An Introduction and Commentary*, vol. 1, Tyndale Old Testament Commentaries (Downers Grove, IL: InterVarsity Press, 1967), 56.

sin nature and possessed no inclination to rebel and disobey God. Fulfilling the mission of making disciples would involve bearing children naturally and teaching and modeling for them how to live in worship and obedience to God. Unfortunately, this was not to be.

The first man and woman, prior to having children, chose to disbelieve God's character, disregard His words, and disobey His expressed will. Nowhere in history can we point to a sinless human parent who led their sinless children to be worshipping, obedient followers of God. The first children born upon the earth were welcomed into this world by fallen parents. And the first parents received into their arms children born with a marred image of God who possessed a fallen nature that opposed God, causing them to be separated from God by sin. God's mission had been interrupted by the pride-filled rebellion of humanity. Natural birth would no longer suffice in multiplying image-bearing followers of God. Human beings do not and cannot naturally live in relationship with God and follow Him.

A supernatural birth is necessary to reproduce image bearers of God who live in relationship with Him. Only when the Spirit of God regenerates the heart of a man or woman can that person be a follower of God, living in right relationship with Him. To be an image-bearing disciple, a person must be born again from above by placing his or her faith in Jesus Christ and His completed work of redemption (Jn 1:13, 3:3). God, in the person and work of His Son Jesus, intervened on our behalf through Christ's death and resurrection to remove the barrier of sin that prevented us from living in relationship with Him (Eph 2:8–9, 2 Cor 5:17). Jesus paid the penalty for our sin and opened the way to new life and relationship with God. Those who trust in Jesus Christ receive the forgiveness of sin and a restored relationship with Him. Now, making disciples in a fallen world occurs when a naturally born individual, who is alienated from God, comes to faith in Jesus Christ, experiencing a new, spiritual birth through the power of the Holy Spirit.

THE GREAT COMMISSION IN THE NEW TESTAMENT

All humanity can once again live in a relationship of worship and obedience to God as a result of Jesus' work. Jesus' mission was to make a way salvation for people to live the life and relationship with God that He purposed before the world was ruined.

After Jesus completed the work for our salvation through His death and resurrection, He gathered His followers together on a hillside where He charged them to go and make disciples of people from every nation, tribe, and language. They were to do so by witnessing to others of the truth of who Jesus is and what He has accomplished by His crucifixion and resurrection (Matt 28:19–20, Luke 24:46–48, Acts 1:8). His instructions reiterated the mission that was instituted from the beginning of creation. Jesus called and commissioned His disciples to be fruitful and multiply more disciples, who in turn would multiply others.[9] In the same way that Adam and Eve had been called and commissioned to be fruitful and multiply, God was entrusting the work of multiplying disciples to those who had trusted in Him by the gospel. Hence, the mission of God has never altered. He always intended for humanity to live in relationship with Him. When the earthly family failed to carry out this task, God brought redemption through Jesus in order to form a new family to carry out His mission. This new family is called the church.

The church is the people gathered together as one family under the rule and reign of Jesus Christ. This new family, being joined together by faith in Jesus, bears responsibility for making disciples.[10] To say that the church has been entrusted to make disciples does not mean that parents have been replaced. Too many Christian parents have wrongly concluded that someone else, namely the corporate church, holds primary responsibility for the mission of making disciples of their children. They abdicate their role and responsibility to vocational Christian workers or volunteers who serve in the local church. Parents

---

[9] Bill Hull, *The Complete Book of Discipleship* (Colorado Springs, CO: NavPress, 2006), 25.

[10] Jim Putnam, *Real Life Discipleship* (Colorado Springs, CO: NavPress, 2010), 19; Mark Dever, *Discipling: How to Help Others Follow Jesus* (Wheaton, IL: Crossway, 2016), 53.

often expect the pastor to lead their children to faith in Jesus Christ and the vocational workers, including small group teachers and other volunteers, to instruct their children to know the Scriptures and how to live them out. This, however, is a gross misunderstanding of what the Scriptures teach.

The New Testament nowhere rescinds the responsibility parents have to lead their children to know and follow God. No amount of combing through the Scriptures will ever produce evidence where God reassigns parents' role and responsibility for making disciples of their children to someone else. John Stott comments, "...Christian parents should jealously guard their responsibility, delegating some of it indeed to both church and school, but never entirely surrendering it. It is their own God-given task; nobody can adequately or completely replace them."[11] God does not permit parents to use the church, school, and government as a substitute or excuse for their delinquency in taking up the mission of God in regard to their children.

The Apostle Paul never saw the church as a replacement for the disciple-making efforts of parents with their children. As he writes to the church in Ephesus, he specifically calls Christian parents, and fathers in particular, to be intentional in the spiritual formation of their children's lives. He writes, "Fathers, do not provoke your children to anger, but bring them up in the discipline and instruction of the Lord" (Eph 6:4).

---

[11] John R. W. Stott, *God's New Society: The Message of Ephesians* (Downers Grove, IL: InterVarsity Press, 1979), 248.

Believing parents are to raise their children in the discipline and instruction of the Lord so that their children may know who God is, what He has done, and how to live in right relationship with Him. For Paul, Christian parents, who are members of Christ's church, still maintain the primary calling of God to engage in the disciple-making efforts with their children. While every member of Christ's church has been tasked with making disciples, Christian parents have been twice commissioned to join in God's mission of multiplying followers of Jesus upon this earth. They have been commissioned as parents in the creation account (Gen 1:28), as well as having received the instruction as followers of Christ and members of His body to make disciples in the New Testament (Matt 28:19–20).

Making disciples is the chief mission of parents in regard to their children. By directing their children to know and follow Jesus Christ, parents engage in leading their children to fulfill the intent for which God made them. But if parents are to make disciples, they must adequately understand how God says disciples are made in Scripture.

HOW TO MAKE A DISCIPLE

God calls, commands, and holds parents accountable for making disciples of their children. But what does it mean to make a disciple? How does the Bible say disciples are made? Making disciples follows four critical steps. These steps include proclaiming the good news, leading others to faith in Jesus Christ, teaching followers of Jesus to grow in worship and obedience to Him, and deploying disciples to make other disciples.

PROCLAIM TO THEM THE GOOD NEWS

Making disciples begins with proclaiming the gospel of Jesus Christ necessary for salvation. John Hendryx concisely defines the gospel, writing, "In short, the Gospel is the life-altering news that Jesus Christ, the eternal Son of God, became man, lived a sinless life under the Law, died for sinners and rose again to reconcile them to himself, eternally victorious over every enemy that stood between God and man."[12] The Apostle Paul declared only through hearing the truth proclaimed about Jesus and His death and resurrection could a person could come to faith (Rom 10:15). Parents who intend to lead their children to be disciples of Jesus Christ must take great care to consistently communicate the gospel to their children.[13] Ken Hemphill and Richard Ross admonish, "No parental duty matters more than introducing one's children to Jesus Christ."[14]

The gospel of Jesus Christ is good news. The gospel is good news because it stands in contrast to the horrible news of

---

[12] John Hendryx, "What is the Gospel?" *Monergism*, No date, accessed September 6, 2019: https://www.monergism.com/ what-gospel-0.

[13] Tedd Tripp and Margy Tripp, *Instructing a Child's Heart* (Wapwallopen, PA: Shepherd Press, 2008), 180.

[14] Ken Hemphill and Richard Ross, *Parenting with Kingdom Purpose* (Nashville, TN: B&H Books, 2005), 40.

the fall. Our disobedience to God has led to a ruined world. Our sin produced a fallen nature and severed our relationship with God. The gospel is the good news that what our sin destroyed can be restored in Jesus Christ. Our children can best understand the beauty of this gospel message when we place it at the heart of the great story of the Scriptures. The Bible communicates one overarching story that follows "four major plot movements—creation, fall, redemption, and restoration."[15]

CREATION – GOD MADE

The great story of Scripture begins with the creation of God. We begin with God, who He is, and what His original plan was for His creation. Our children should learn that there is one God who is eternal, all-powerful, all wise, and perfectly good. He eternally exists as Father, Son, and Holy Spirit (Matt 28:19–20, Jn 14:16–17). In the beginning, the Triune God created all things pure and perfect (Gen 1:31). He made all things by Himself and for Himself. Nothing came to exist without Him (Jn 1:1–3, Acts 4:24). In all of God's work, human beings were the greatest work of His creation. God made humanity in His image to reflect His likeness in the world. He made us for a relationship in which we were intended to enjoy Him forever through worship and obedience. He created us so that He too

---

[15] Bruce Ashford, ed., *Theology and Practice of Mission: God, the Church, and the Nations* (Nashville, Tenn.: B&H Academic, 2011), 6.

could delight and enjoy us forever as we lived willfully under His rule and reign as King (Gen 1:26, Is 62:4, 1 Pet 2:9–10).

THE FALL – HUMANITY RUINED

Human beings were placed in the perfect creation of God to live in relationship with Him. God placed us in this world to live in worship and obedience to Him. Yet, we chose to rebel rather than worship and obey. Instead of submitting to Him, we sinned against Him. Greg Gilbert reminds us that sin is "the breaking of a relationship, and even more, it is a rejection of God himself—a repudiation of God's rule, God's care, God's authority, and God's right to command those to whom he gave life."[16] When Adam and Eve violated the character and sovereignty of God by their intentional disobedience, they ushered in ruin to God's creation. Their choice to delight in something other than God and to disobey God's command brought the whole world into chaos and under a curse from God. Death, violence, sickness, broken relationships, and all manner of destruction that exists today were ushered in because Adam and Eve, and all humanity, chose to sin against God (Rom 3:23, 5:12–19).

Sin destroyed the world, and it decimated the relationship we were meant and made to enjoy with God. John Stott observes that even though "[m]an's highest destiny is to know

---

[16] Greg Gilbert, *What is the Gospel?* Wheaton, IL: Crossway, 2010), 48.

God and to be in personal relationship with God," the reality is that the most grievous of "sin's consequences is that it estranges us from God."[17] Our own actions have led us to be separated from God with no way to return on our own.

Our children cannot grasp the importance of the gospel and their need to trust in Jesus Christ until they realize that they are born estranged from God because of their sin. Though they were made to be in relationship with God, they now live separated from God because of disobedience. They have a sinful nature that leads them to sin habitually because of the evil nature within them (Jam 1:14). They possess no desire or ability to do otherwise. Sin has caused them, along with all humanity, to live in darkness, having been blinded by Satan. They are unable to see the light of the glory and greatness of Jesus Christ until God opens our eyes to the truth (2 Cor 4:4). In this place of sin and rebellion, they deserve the rightful wrath of God against their wrongdoing (Eph 2:1–3). The future of every sinful human being is the certain judgment of God unless someone intervenes to rescue us (Matt 25:41–46). Without rescue, our children and we are all traveling the broad path to destruction that leads to an eternal existence of separation from God. All who enter that place will experience the anguish and torment for our rejection of and rebellion against Him (Matt 7:13–14; 21–23).

---

[17] John Stott, *Basic Christianity* (Chicago, IL: Inter-Varsity Press, 1964), 72.

REDEMPTION – CHRIST RESTORES

When our children come to understand that they are excluded from relationship with God and subjects of His judgment, they begin to grasp their need for forgiveness of sin and restoration of their broken relationship with God. This is why the gospel is good news. The gospel delivers hope. God inserted Himself into our world in the person of Jesus Christ to solve our problem. Instead of casting humanity aside in our sin and leaving us without hope, God sent His Son into the mess we made to rescue us. God pursued us out of His great love for us, because He desires and delights to have relationship with us.

God sent His Son—fully God and fully man—to live the life we should have lived (Lk 1:31–32, Gal 4:4–5). Jesus lived in a relationship of perfect worship and obedience to God the Father (Jn 8:28–29). The life Adam and Eve and all humanity failed to live was perfectly fulfilled in Jesus Christ. He met the standard of perfection required to be a worthy sacrifice. He then died the death we should have suffered. He absorbed in His body upon the cross God's wrath against every act of disobedience and rebellion we committed. Jesus was the perfect sacrifice dying in the place of guilty sinners. As God, Jesus satisfied the criteria of a perfect sacrifice. As a man, Jesus fit the condition as a suitable substitute for humanity. After His death, He rose again from to offer new life and relationship with

God to us. Because of this, we can once again have a relationship of worship and obedience with Him.

The Apostle Paul summed up the good news in this way, saying, "Christ died for our sins, according to the Scriptures, was buried and rose again the third day, according to the Scriptures" (1 Cor 15:3-4). Jesus died on purpose for us. Christ, the One righteous, gave Himself for the many unrighteous, in order to remove the sin of offense that stood between God and us. As a result, when we place our faith in Jesus and His completed work of salvation, we receive forgiveness and the reconciliation of relationship to God (Rom 5:8). God's work in Jesus aimed to reconcile "the world to himself, not counting [our] trespasses against [us]..." (2 Cor 5:19). The gospel gives hope to human beings ruined by their own deeds.

RESTORATION – KINGDOM COME

Finally, the Scripture declares that God's redemption of sinners is part building and establishing His kingdom. The kingdom of God is about His rule and reign. Through Jesus, God redeems a people to live under His reign. Yet they live in a place that often exists seemingly under the reign of a usurper, Satan and sinful human beings. However, one day God will restore all things to be under His rule and reign.

A complete, future restoration is coming in which God will set things right just as they were in His creation before the fall.

God promises that one-day a new heaven and new earth will be fixed in place where there is no more disobedience, evil, or brokenness (Rev 21:27). In that place, God will once again make His dwelling among people. No more will we live by faith. For there, we will live in His presence to worship and obey Him forever. He will rule and reign as King over the kingdom of people He has rescued and in the place that He has established where sin and His enemies have been eradicated. Those who have trusted in Jesus Christ anticipate this future; a future when we no longer walk by faith but live in the presence of God, seeing the very One whom our soul loves (Is 66:22–23; Revelation 20). We look forward with anticipation to a new home where the peace of God that was shattered through man's rebellion is restored. We long for no more chaos, death, destruction, suffering, and pain in a world cleansed of all unrighteousness of sin and its consequences.

This future restoration is something we must remind our children of as part of the good news of what God is doing. As we teach our children of the completed work of Jesus' death and resurrection for our salvation, we still point them to the final act of that salvation in the future promise God has made of a new heaven and new earth where God reigns with His people. We teach our children to cling tightly to this hope amidst the suffering, trials, and hardships of the present sin-racked world. We remind them that the gospel calls us to live in worship and obedience to Jesus Christ as citizens of His kingdom rather than mere residents of this afflicted world. Our allegiance is to Christ the King more than any earthly authority or ruler.

Teaching our children to hope in God's future restoration of a new heaven and new earth over which He will eternally rule and reign directs them away from living as though this life and world is the ultimate end. The eternal future of every follower of Jesus is living in God's presence to worship and obey Him forever. This truth points them beyond the temporal pleasures of this world. Instead of living for momentary thrills and satisfaction, God calls us to raise our affections to focus on eternal pleasures and treasures in Jesus Christ. Parents should aim to direct the affections of their children's hearts to the things in which God delights. Directing our children to pursue earthly riches, power, or success, which all disappear at the doorway of eternity, is to encourage them to exchange true treasure for trash. The more our children long for the promise that God will reconcile all things to Himself and under His reign, the more they will live here on earth as sons and daughters of the King who have citizenship in a kingdom greater than this world (1 Pet 1:3–9).

PROCLAIM IN WORD AND DEED

Proclaiming the gospel as the good news at the heart of God's great story in Scripture is the first step in leading our children to be disciples of Jesus Christ. We cannot overlook that the gospel is not merely words to be declared but also a witness of one's life to be displayed. The verbal testimony of the life-transforming power of Jesus Christ through His death and resurrection gains credibility and power when it flows from the life of one who thinks as with the mind of Christ, speaks as with the lips of Christ, and acts as with the hands and feet of Christ. No doubt this was what the Apostle John partly had in mind when he instructed believers to love both in word and deed as evidence of the gospel having transformed them from the inside out (1 Jn 3:18). If we speak of the love, grace, and mercy of Jesus Christ, but fail to evidence the same in our words and actions, our words are likely to fall on skeptical or deaf ears.

We are always communicating, even when we are not speaking any words. If as parents we display an alternate message to the gospel, then our effort to point our children to faith in Jesus Christ will be severely hindered, if not fail. One way we send conflicting messages is to preach a gospel of love and grace and yet live in practice a message of condemnation and human works or achievement. Another way is that we teach our children to trust in Jesus Christ for salvation and eternal life in heaven and then direct them to live as their own gods in pursuit of their own plans in this world. The gospel is not good news of the life we will live after this life. The gospel is the radical reformation to live in this world the life God made us to enjoy. Our work as parents to proclaim the gospel to our children requires we examine both the declaration of our lips and the display of lives to insure that both align with the truth of God's Word.

LEAD THEM TO FAITH IN JESUS CHRIST

The second step in making a disciple is leading others to faith in Jesus Christ. Proclaiming the truth about who Jesus Christ is and what He has done for our redemption must occur first. Faith in Christ comes through hearing the Word of God (Rom 10:15). Our children benefit from hearing the gospel regularly proclaimed to them, coupled with an invitation to trust by faith in Jesus. Churches should present the gospel message clearly in their corporate gatherings and invite hearers to response in faith and repentance. Yet parents cannot and should not rely solely upon the worship gatherings of the local church to be sufficient to do so alone.

Parents have a responsibility to intentionally lead their children to hear and understand the gospel. As our children hear and understand the gospel, though, we cannot think that it is enough to know the truth or facts about God and the gospel (Js 2:19). Trusting in Jesus Christ by faith as a result of hearing the good news proclaimed is what brings a person to be in reconciled relationship with God. The purpose for which Jesus came was to reconcile sinners to Himself no matter how far they are from God. All Christians, including Christian parents, have been tasked with the ministry of seeing individuals reconciled to God by proclaiming the gospel and leading individuals to trust in Christ.

The Apostle Paul wrote that followers of Jesus have a God-given assignment to carry out the ministry of reconciliation. The ministry of reconciliation is God's work through His followers to lead sinners far from Him back into a right relationship with Him through faith in Jesus. This ministry has been assigned to us as Jesus' followers. We have been entrusted with the gospel to be His ambassadors. We share the good news with others and invite them to trust in Jesus. God works to use our sharing of the gospel and the invitation we extend to others to believe in Jesus to lead people to surrender their lives by faith to follow Jesus in new life and relationship with Him (2 Cor 5:20). Our relationship with God is only restored through faith in Jesus because only Jesus' death and resurrection constructed the necessary bridge that connects humanity back into relationship with God again. As parents, engaging in the ministry of reconciliation with our children demands that we call them to turn from themselves and the wicked inclinations of their hearts and turn in faith to trust and follow Jesus Christ through His death and resurrection (Mk 1:15, Acts 16:31, Rom 10:9–10). No parent can make the decision of faith for his or her children. But we can share the gospel and lead them to place their faith in

Jesus who "is able to save to the uttermost those who draw near to God through him…" (Heb 7:25).

TEACH THEM TO GROW IN JESUS CHIRST

When our children turn away from sin and trust in Jesus Christ alone for salvation, they have not come to the end of their journey. A decision to follow Jesus is the starting block of the Christian life, not the finish line. This means that a parent's work of making disciples of their children has not concluded when their children surrender to Jesus. Our children must grow as His disciples. This requires parents who walk alongside of their children daily, instructing them from the Scriptures to know and obey the commands of Christ.

Jesus declared that making disciples involves more than leading a person to utter a prayer of salvation. For sure, a person moves from death to life by confessing and repenting of his or her sin and trusting in Jesus Christ. Through faith in Jesus, God converts the sinner into a saint. Faith in Jesus converts an individual into a disciple, but only continued growth in obedience to Jesus Christ matures one as a disciple. From the moment our children receive God's gift of salvation, God intends that they grow in "the grace and knowledge" of Him (2 Pet 3:18). This occurs through teaching them to obey all that He has commanded (Matt 28:20). The way to becoming like Christ, reflecting Him in greater ways, is through a life shaped to fit the standard of God's Word.

Teaching disciples to obey God's truth occurs best when communicated within relationship.[18] Relationship provides the place and opportunity to communicate the truth. Even more, relationship brings the needed accountability to obey the truth as a believer. The parent-child relationship offers the best structure for children to learn to obey the commands of Jesus with proper accountability. This does not mean that this is the only relationship children can or should have for learning God's truth and having others hold them responsible to obey His instructions. Rather, the parent-child relationship is the primary relationship for this. It is so because God established it for this purpose. Every new follower of Jesus Christ, in order to grow in Christ, must be taught to obey Jesus' commands in a relationship of accountability. Without such, no disciple, our children included, will be able to grow fully in the relationship of worship and obedience for which Christ created them.

TEACHING THEM TO PUT OFF AND PUT ON

Teaching our children as disciples to obey the commands of Jesus focuses toward helping them to see what to put off of the old desires and deeds of the flesh and what to put on of the new life they have received in Christ (Eph 4:22–24). The message of

---

[18] See Josh McDowell and Thomas Williams, *The Relational Word* (Holiday, FL: Green Key Books, 2006).

the Christian life is not simply what we can no longer do, but rather what God desires and empowers us to do for His glory. Wayne Mack writes, "For our instruction to be biblically accurate, we must not merely tell people what they should not do but also what they should do, and vice versa. We need to help them replace old, sinful habits with godly ones."[19]

Again, parents are best positioned and capable of doing this. As we walk alongside our children daily, we have the ability to observe their lives close up. We see the areas in their lives where they struggle and sin. We understand where they fail to deny themselves and to put off what displeases and disobeys God. With love, humility, and grace, we can direct our children to see these areas and point them to the life God intended. God has outlined in the Bible the life that is good, right, and pleasing to Him. Parents direct their children to this life by teaching God's Word and encouraging them that the power of Christ is at work in them to enable them to live it out. God enables Christians to replace the sinful works of the flesh with the fruit of the Spirit whom he has placed to dwell inside of us (Gal 5:16–26). Yet we must help our children know that the work of putting off the old life and putting on the new life in Christ is not a work that happens without their involvement. Our must know how the divine power of God's Spirit works

---

[19] Wayne Mack, "Providing Instruction through Biblical Counseling," *Counseling: How to Counsel Biblically* (Nashville, TN: Thomas Nelson, 2005), 170.

through the personal discipline of their own life in order to cultivate godliness (Matt 3:8, Phil 2:12–13, 1 Tim 4:7).

Too often believers can view justification as all the work of God and sanctification as all the work of man. This is not biblically accurate. God rescues us from sin and continues to work to present us worthy of the gospel that has saved us. Paul wrote, "[I]t is God who works in you, both to will and to work for his good pleasure" (Phil 2:13). Just prior to this verse, Paul calls Christians to work out their own salvation through faithful obedience. Salvation is the work of God to redeem us into right relationship with Him. Paul is not suggesting we can work to earn our salvation. To the contrary, he is affirming that those who have been saved "by grace" and "not of works" will produce obedience to Christ as masterpieces of His redeeming love (Eph 2:8–10). Like James who argued that good works give evidence of salvation (Js 2:18), so Paul is instructing Christians to show their salvation and grow in their salvation through obedience and good deeds. Thus, we are to discipline ourselves in order that our lives may be lived in greater conformity to the life of Christ we have been redeemed to live. Paul says, however, that God works in us to will and to do what pleases Him. Having received salvation as the free gift of God, we are then to live out our salvation in godly thought, speech, action, and motives. But we cannot do this on our own. We put off evil and put on godliness because of the inward work of God by His Spirit. He works in us "to will and to work for his pleasure." This demands that we surrender and yield our lives to the Spirit dwelling in us. We are desperate to be filled with greater fullness of His Spirit that leads to greater submission to the Spirit's power and influence in our lives (Acts 13:52, Eph 5:18). God will produce in us what He desires by His power. But our sanctification, our being set apart from this world and being transformed to be like Jesus Christ, will not occur without our cooperation and discipline.

Parents, therefore, lead their children well when they teach them that God works in our lives through His Spirit coupled with our personal discipline as Christians. Growing in holiness demands that they know the role and necessity of discipline, obedience, and dying daily to themselves daily in order to live more fully under the rule and reign of Jesus Christ. God will work and empower our children to put off ungodliness and put on Christlikeness as they yield to the Spirit's inner working and cultivate personal discipline by laying aside sin and encumbrances in order to pursue the holiness of Christ (Heb 12:1).

TEACHING THEM THE MOTIVATION FOR CHANGE

The motivation to pursue holiness comes from the overwhelming, inexpressible grace God has poured out upon us. We do not merely engage in trying to put off the works of the flesh and put on the life of Christ out of duty. The desire to be continually changed into Christ-likeness should flow out of gratitude for the redemption of God in our lives. Every believer must bear this in mind as he or she wrestles long and hard with the personal sin that entangles his or her heart and life. Tedd and Margy Tripp write, "Help your children to see that the motivation for obedience is the amazing grace of God in the gospel. We were just as bad as everyone else in the world. But then the goodness and mercy of God appeared." This is what we read in the Scriptures. They go on to add:

> The chief way the apostles motivated Christians to obey God was to emphasize God's grace, kindness, mercy, love and free forgiveness through the cross. The more that believing children grow in their understanding of the free forgiveness of God and the full righteousness of Christ given to all who embrace Jesus by faith alone, the more they will grow in holiness.[20]

THREE WAYS TO ENGAGE IN TEACHING

Our children must learn to hear and obey the commands of Jesus Christ as they grow up in Him as disciples. Parents stand in the primary role for doing so with their children. We must be intentional and strategic in this effort. We must seek the times and places where we can instruct our children from God's Word and guide them to put His truth into practice. While a number of ways exist for parents to guide their children into the knowledge of the truth, there are three specific ways every parent can and

---

[20] Tripp and Tripp, *Instructing a Child's Heart*, 186–187.

should engage in this work. Parents can impress the Word of God upon the hearts of their children and lead them to greater obedience to Christ through family worship, consistent and loving discipline, and using the teaching moments that abound in the circumstances of everyday life.

TEACHING THROUGH FAMILY WORSHIP

One practical and powerful way parents can engage in teaching their children to know and obey Christ's commands is through an intentional, structured family devotion and worship time. Family worship in the home makes a positive impact on the whole family, especially the children. This time focuses the whole family on God and His glory. It also calls each person to worship and obey Jesus Christ, educates the family in the truth of God, focuses on growing in obedience as disciples, and equips and prepares the family for corporate worship.[21] Many parents, however, feel overwhelmed when they think of leading family worship.

While family worship should not be regarded flippantly or taken lightly, this does not mean that a time of family worship must be a complicated undertaking that requires lengthy planning. *First,* set a time and place for family worship. Schedules may require flexibility, though parents should seek as

---

[21] See Jason Helopoulos, "11 Reasons to Worship with Your Family," *The Gospel Coalition*, March 8, 2011, accessed December 10, 2019: https://www.thegospelcoalition.org/article/11-reasons-to-worship-with-your-family/.

often as possible to maintain consistency both in having family worship, as well as when and where this time occurs. *Second,* plan the time to include three basic elements: Reading Scripture, prayer, and singing a song or hymn of praise to God.

The first element of family worship is reading the Word of God together. Scripture is the written revelation of God to us. By reading His Word, we know how we are to rightly respond to Him. Parents should read the Scripture during family worship and guide the family to discuss what the Scripture means and how to apply the truth in personal, practical ways. As children get older, you can incorporate them into leading the family worship with you by having them read the Bible or provide questions to discuss. Allowing older children at times to lead the family worship also trains them to do so with their children in the years to come.

The second element of family worship is a time of prayer. Times of prayer should celebrate the greatness of God, include confession of sin, express thanksgiving to God for His many works, and make requests for the needs of one another in the family as well as those outside the family. Additionally, the Scripture read during family worship should be incorporated into the prayer time. This is a way to teach our children to bring the truth of God's Word into our prayer times, speaking back to God the truth He has proclaimed to us. Prayer times in family worship also become a tool for teaching children how to pray.

Most believers learn to pray from listening to others pray and then modeling their prayers after them.

A final element of family worship can be to sing a simple song of praise and worship to God. Singing during family worship does not require instrumentation, a skilled musician, or a trained vocalist. Singing together is far less about the quality of the singing and far more about the act of lifting our voices together as a sacrifice of praise to God (Ps 150, Heb 13:15). Singing the truths of God's Word also enables children to remember His truth and have it imprinted upon their hearts.

TEACHING THROUGH DISCIPLINE

Another way parents instill truth into the hearts and lives of their children is through loving, consistent discipline. Parents should encourage children to discipline themselves. Yet our children also require we guide them in this process by bringing discipline into their lives. The word *discipline* comes from the same root as the word *disciple*.[22]

Discipline is a necessary part of the process of making and becoming a disciple. The discipline parents bring in their children's lives prior to their children coming to faith in Jesus Christ exposes them to their need for salvation. As parents lead their children to see and acknowledge their sin, they help them

---

[22] Richard Patterson Jr., *Parenting: Loving Our Children with God's Love: 9 Studies for Individuals or Groups: With Notes for Leaders*, A LifeGuide Bible Study (Downers Grove, IL: IVP Connect, 2006), 28.

to understand the deep need they have for salvation and forgiveness. The consequences for disobedience we give our children points to the necessity of punishment for sin and disobedience. That a required payment for the penalty of sin is required elevates the centrality of why Christ died on the cross for sinners.

When parents discipline their children after they have come to follow Jesus Christ, their discipline benefits their children by helping them to identify the areas of their lives where surrender and obedience to Jesus are lacking. When children disobey in attitude, word, or action, a parent's loving discipline becomes a means of "teaching children character, self-control, and moral behavior."[23] A believing child who receives discipline is redirected away from what is in error to God's will and commends them to what exemplifies God's will. But children who err without discipline lose out on invaluable teaching that leads them to worship and obey God in a greater way. Those who do not receive godly discipline miss moments where the grace and truth of God could powerfully transform their hearts and lives.

---

[23] K. V. Cook, "Child Discipline," ed. David G. Benner and Peter C. Hill, Baker Encyclopedia of Psychology & Counseling, Baker Reference Library (Grand Rapids, MI: Baker Books, 1999), 182.

TEACHING IN THE CIRCUMSTANCES OF LIFE

All parents have innumerable teaching moments with their children afforded to them everyday. The majority of teaching parents will do with our children will take place in informal rather than formal settings. Daily we find ourselves in situations, circumstances, and conversations with our children that provide ample occasion for us to help our children see the world through biblical lenses. These times arise not according to plan or structure. They occur in the car or at dinner with friends. They happen in regard to homework, plans with friends, or a sporting event. No matter when, where, or how they occur, these times present prime points for teaching our children about the nature who God is, what He has commanded, and how they can live in a manner pleasing to Him. These teaching moments do not occur just when our children mess up or do wrong. Good and bad times allow us to impart truth to our children, either through affirmation or correction. We must seize these opportunities to impress God's truth on their hearts and help them be shaped by Scripture. When we do, "[l]ife becomes the classroom of discipleship, and class is always in session."[24]

THE GOAL OF OUR TEACHING

In all of our teaching, the goal of parents is to see that their children live in greater worship and obedience to Jesus Christ

---

[24] Robby Gallaty, *Rediscovering Discipleship: Making Jesus' Final Words Our First Work* (Grand Rapids, MI: Zondervan, 2015), 82.

by knowing and obeying His commands. Our teaching aims to lead our children to be disciples who are maturing into "the measure of the stature of the fullness of Christ" (Eph 4:13).

DEPLOY DISCIPLE-MAKING DISCIPLES

The final step in making a disciple is deploying him or her as a follower of Jesus to multiply other disciples. Bill Hull charges, "Jesus told us to be disciples and to make disciples."[25] That is, we are to be disciple-making disciples. We are not to be the beneficiaries of another Christian's disciple-making efforts and yet refuse to engage in making disciples of others. Jesus expects us to reproduce other disciples. The gospel came to us that it may flow through us to others. God brought others to grow us as a disciple that we would walk with others in growing as a disciple.

A disciple is a follower of Jesus who is "intentionally equipped with the Word of God through accountable relationships empowered by the Holy Spirit" in order to then go and "replicate faithful followers of Christ."[26] Any follower of Jesus who fails to replicate faithful followers of Jesus Christ has short-circuited the discipleship process. He or she has also misunderstood the heart and mission of God. Every Christian is to be a missionary in God's disciple-making mission.

---

[25] Hull, *The Complete Book of Discipleship,* 25.
[26] Robby Gallaty, "We Must Replicate Disciples," *Replicate*, February 27, 2015, accessed online December 30, 2019: https://replicate.org/we-must-replicate-disciples/.

Making disciples of our children requires that we teach and equip them to advance the gospel and increase disciples on the earth for Christ's glory. We must prepare them to actively share the gospel and lead others to faith in Jesus Christ. We must help them to know how to teach new believers to grow in worship and obedience to Jesus Christ through obedience to His commands. And then, we must release our children to go and make disciples.

Parents often fail to take responsibility for proclaiming the gospel to their children and leading them to faith in Jesus. But parents fail all the more to instruct their children that they have been redeemed to take part in God's mission. Too often parents do not teach their children that as Jesus' followers they have been given the task of multiplying disciples. Rarely today do Christian parents raise their children to release them to advance God's mission wherever He may direct them. Andrew Murray offers this critique, writing, "Simply, Christian parents do not, as a rule, educate their children that they are the Lord's, place them at His disposal, or train them to look upon this as their highest privilege."[27]

God has enlisted every follower of Jesus, regardless of vocation, to making disciples in his or her location.[28] Murray

---

[27] Andrew Murray, *How to Raise Children for Christ* (Abbotsford, WI: Aneko Press, 2016), 60–61.

[28] See Kent and Davidene Humphreys, *Show and Then Tell* (Chicago, IL: Moody Press, 2000), 21–31;

adds, "...[E]very believer has been called to give his life to God's service and to win others to His knowledge..."[29] We ought to teach our children to see their vocation as a place and means of advancing God's kingdom through making disciples. Every reputable and godly vocation is a location for loving God and loving other people as part of God's mission to proclaim the gospel and lead them to know, follow, and grow in Jesus Christ.[30] The greatest love we can demonstrate toward another person is love for his or her soul that leads us to share the gospel with them in order that they can be in relationship with God again.

We must never insinuate or overtly teach that God's mission of making disciples is reserved for an elite group of individuals who serve in positions of vocational Christian service. Rather, we need to impress upon our children that the responsibility for God's mission of making disciples rests upon every follower of Jesus Christ. Until we observe this teaching and practice of Jesus reflected in our children's lives, we cannot

---

[29] Andrew Murray, *Walking with God: The Andrew Murray Trilogy on Sanctification* (Gene Fedele, ed.; Alachua, FL: Bridge-Logos, 2008), 202.

[30] See Gene Veith, *God at Work* (Wheaton, IL: Crossway, 2002). In this work, Veith reminds the reader that the Latin word for "vocation" is the word for "calling." He asserts that a tragic issue that has occurred has been the sharp distinction in the minds of many Christians who regard some vocations as sacred, while others are determined to be secular. Instead, Veith challenges us as followers of Jesus Christ to see every honorable vocation as a person's place of calling to live out the purpose of our vocation. He articulates that the purpose of our "vocation is to love and serve one's neighbor" out of one's love for God birthed in him or her through salvation in Jesus Christ (p. 39–40). He identifies the chief means of loving one's neighbor as leading him or her to faith in Jesus to become a disciple.

claim to have reproduced the kind of disciples Jesus intended (2 Tim 2:1–2).

Every vocation is a location for living on mission with God. Parents should never dissuade their children from following God in vocational Christian service just because Christians can serve God and make disciples regardless of his or her vocation. Christian parents are susceptible, along with unbelieving parents, to press their children to pursue an education and occupation that is deemed respectable by the world. We can encourage our children to choose a vocational path that will produce greater earthly wealth and benefits. Again, Murray challenges parents, saying,

> Let us devote every child to God and His service. Let us cease praying that our children may be saved, while never think of giving them to serve. Let us cease choosing honorable and lucrative professions for our children, with the truth that they can serve God in any calling, allowing that to be an excuse for declining special service. Let us lay each child upon the altar, seeking this one thing—that he may become worthy and fit for the service of the King."[31]

DO NOT DESPAIR

Having discussed what it means to make a disciple, the task of being the primary disciple-maker of our children may sound daunting. In short, it should. Making disciples is indeed a noble and great task. The work is hard, challenging, and relentless. But we need not despair.

---

[31] Murray, *How to Raise Children for Christ*, 60–61.

We must remember and take courage in the fact that God has given us everything necessary to carry out what He called us to do. He has not asked any parent to make disciples of their children, leaving them alone to do so. God promises and provides the resources required to make disciples of Jesus. In the next chapter, we will see the supernatural provision of God given to us so that we can fulfill our calling and responsibility as the primary faith-trainers in our children's lives.

CHAPTER 3

THE CHIEF HELP IN THE MISSION

Sundar Singh planned to end his life by stepping in front of the morning train. The fourteen-year-old young man's distress started with the death of his mother. Though he had been born into a Sikh family in northern India, Sundar's mother introduced him to Christianity. She even enrolled him in a Christian school. So when she died, he blamed the Christian God for her death. At school, Sundar "threw filth on his Christian teachers, mocked their Scriptures, and interrupted classes."[1] In an ultimate show of disregard and disgust for Christianity and the God of the Bible, he burned a copy of the Bible page by page. None of this brought comfort for young Sundar and, as he wrestled with the anguish in his soul, he decided he would end his life.

On the night before he intended to commit suicide, Sundar sat in his room and prayed that the real God would appear to him. If God did not appear, he determined he would step onto

---

[1] "Sundar Singh's Vision of Christ," *Christianity.com*, May 3, 2010, accessed online August 12, 2019, https://www.christianity.com/church/church-history/timeline/1901-2000/sundar-singhs-vision-of-christ-11630674.html.

the train tracks to be killed by the five o'clock morning train. An encounter with Jesus Christ, that night, changed Sundar's life forever. In answer to his prayer, Sundar witnessed a glow in the room. He saw a figure standing in the center of the ever-growing bright light. The figure spoke, saying, "How long will you persecute ME? I have come to save you. You were praying to know the right way. Why do you not take it? I am the Way."[2] Falling to his knees, he prayed for Jesus Christ to forgive his sin and transform his life.

God rescued Sundar from both his present despair and future destruction through faith in Jesus Christ. In spite of his family's fierce opposition, Sundar was baptized as a declaration that he was a follower of Jesus. His family was doubly opposed to his desire to share with others the message of hope in Jesus Christ. Undeterred, Sundar gave the rest of his life to join God in his mission of making disciples. He devoted himself to leading others to faith in Christ and teaching believers to live in worship and obedience to Him. Yet, his work of making disciples came with much adversity.

Oftentimes, the hardships Sundar faced forced him to acknowledge that his own strength and ability were insufficient for the task. Over and over again, he witnessed God's sufficiency to supply him with everything he needed to be obedient to fulfill God's mission. An example of this occurred

---

[2] Janet Benge and Geoff Benge, *Sundar Singh: Footprints Over the Mountains* (Seattle, WA: YWAM Publishing, 2005), 31.

during one of his many missionary journeys. Sundar asked a group of individuals for directions to the nearest village, but the people intentionally gave him wrong information. The path they told him to take was both dangerous and deadly. As night began to fall, Sundar arrived at the bank of an icy river. With the sound of wild animals about him and the swift flowing water before him, he knew he could not turn back. He would need to try to cross the river. He tried unsuccessfully and, having failed, he "sat down in despair, feeling that things boded ill for [him] that day and that the end of [his] life was at hand."[3]

With tears filling his eyes, Sundar looked up to see a man sitting by a fire on the opposite side of the riverbank. The man called out saying, "Don't worry, I'm coming to help you." Sundar then watched as the man fearlessly and effortlessly crossed the river. He then instructed Sundar, saying, "Sit on my shoulders–don't be afraid." Sundar ascended the man's back and sat perched on the man's shoulders as he waded through the river. Having crossed the river, the man walked up the bank and placed Sundar down.[4] Sundar turned to express his gratitude to the man and "preach the Gospel to him," but "…when [he] turned and looked back, immediately the fire and the man disappeared…"[5]

[3] A. J. Appasamy, *Sundar Singh* (Cambridge, England: The Lutterworth Press, 1958), 51.

[4] Phyllis Thompson, *Sadhu Sundar Singh: A Biography of the Remarkable Indian Disciple of Jesus Christ* (Singapore: Armour Publishing, 2005), 73–74.

[5] Appasamy, *Sundar Singh*, 51.

Sundar believed and reported this story throughout the rest of his life, declaring that God had sent the help he needed to cross the river so he could continue his work. In spite of others plotting for his harm, God gave Sundar what his human strength could not produce so he could advance the mission of making disciples. When he found himself in need or faced his own feelings of inadequacy, Sundar looked to an all-powerful and all-sufficient God fully willing and able to meet His need.[6]

God always equips and enables those He calls. No matter the task or the difficulty thereof, God amply gives what we need to be faithful and obedient to Him. This is equally true for parents whom God has called to lead their children to know and follow Jesus. For this God-given role and assignment, God provides the equipping and enabling needed for parents to faithfully and effectively accomplish this mission even when they feel inadequate.

FEELING INADEQUATE

Most Christian parents affirm that they have the primary responsibility for the spiritual formation of their children's lives. At the same time, they often express that they are inadequate or incapable of fulfilling this mission.[7] Christian

---

[6] Benge and Benge, *Sundar Singh,* 50–51.

[7] "Parents Accept Responsibility for Their Child's Spiritual Development But Struggle With Effectiveness," *Barna Group*, May 6, 2003, accessed 5 September 2019: https://www.barna.com/research/parents-accept-responsibility-for-their-childs-spiritual-development-but-struggle-with-effectiveness/.

parents may feel inferior in making disciples because they compare themselves to other parents. They may believe themselves incapable of leading their children to be mature followers of Jesus because they compare their knowledge and training to that of vocational Christian workers whom they deem to be more qualified. In some cases, parents' feelings of inferiority could stem from their not having witnessed their own parents carry out the task of make disciples of them or modeling what that looks like in the home when they were children. No matter the reason parents feel incapable or inadequate, the reality is that too many are charting into unknown waters they feel unfit to navigate.

The failure of many local churches to equip and encourage parents in discipling their children certainly has not infused parents with courage or conviction to step up and take the spiritual leadership of their children's lives. Parents tend to rely on vocational Christian workers to take the responsibility God gave to fathers and mothers. They begin to see seminary-trained, church staff as professionals who are qualified and capable of sharing the gospel with their children, leading them to faith, and teaching them to obey His commands.[8] A large

---

[8] Ray Ortlund, "Brothers, we are not professionals," *The Gospel Coalition*, February 18, 2013, accessed August 6, 2019, https://www.thegospelcoalition.org/blogs/ray-ortlund/brothers-we-are-not-professionals/; John Piper, *Brothers, We Are Not Professionals* (Nashville, TN: B&H Books, 2013). In the article by Ray Ortlund, he addresses the reissue of John Piper's book by the same title as his article. Ortlund argues, as does Piper in his book, against the professionalization of pastoral and vocational ministry. Even more, they both admonish pastors and

number of parents state that they are unable to be the primary ones to exercise spiritual leadership in the faith formation of their children.[9]

GOD'S DIVINE HELP

The sense of inadequacy among so many parents to make disciples of their children exists for good reason. After all, as we stated before, making disciples is not a quick work that comes with ease. Even more, the work of making disciples is a task God has entrusted to us that we cannot accomplish on our own. When we realize we are incapable of making disciples in our own strength, wisdom, and efforts, why would we not experience some level of fear and insecurity? As parents, we can easily despair that the task is too great and our resources too small. But when we understand we cannot do what God has asked of us on our own, our desperation can propel us beyond ourselves to an utter dependence upon Him who is the source and supply of all we need (2 Cor 9:8).

---

clergy to refrain from presenting themselves as professionals or pursuing the advancement of vocational ministry to a place of professional respectability. Tragically, there has been a professionalization of vocational, pastoral ministry to the degree that many Christians and church members consider clergy as professionals who should be employed or tasked with matters, such as the discipleship of one's own children, instead of assuming that responsibility entrusted by God to us as parents.

[9] Janice Haywood, *Enduring Connections: Creating a Preschool and Children's Ministry* (St. Louis, MO: Chalice Press, 2007), 26; Carroll Anne Sheppard and Nancy Burton Dilliplane, *Congregational Connections: Uniting Six Generations in the Church* (Bloomington, IN: Xlibris, 2011), 81.

Crawford Loritts encourages believers to see God's purpose in the times and tasks where they feel overwhelmed and incapable of doing what God asks. He writes:

> There is always a gap between what you have and what God wants done. You won't always see how it can be done. And so you're faced with a choice. Either you allow the magnitude of the challenge to overwhelm you, or you surrender all your deficiencies to Him, acknowledging that the *only* way you can accomplish the assignment is if He does it through you.

He goes on to encourage believers that when God uses us to do what we could not do on our own, God receives the glory and praise for what He accomplishes through us. He adds:

> It's good to be reminded that we are most useful to God when we realize that in our selves we don't have what it takes to get His assignments done. The reason we are inadequate is because God wants us and everybody else to know that what has been accomplished has been done in His strength and for His glory.[10]

This is great encouragement for the parent who feels inadequate to fulfill the role of spiritual leadership with their children. God has given us the overwhelming task of leading our children to be disciples of Jesus Christ, but He gives us what we need and works through us to accomplish what He wants done.

God never intended for any of His followers to do His will or work in human wisdom and power. Seeking to do what God asks on our own ends in failure and frustration every time. God never demands of us anything for which He will not amply

---

[10] Crawford Loritts, *Leadership as an Identity* (Chicago, IL: Moody Publishers, 2009), 39–40.

supply to us all we require for the task (2 Pet 1:3, Phil 4:19). He has not left us helpless. He promises and provides the power and resources we need as His people to accomplish what He calls and holds us accountable to do. For this reason, parents can be confident that God has not left them without the divine help necessary to be faithful and obedient in the God-given assignment of leading their children to know and follow Jesus Christ.

God supplies four essential resources to parents to provide what they need in order to lead their children to live as followers of Jesus in a lifetime of worship and obedience to Him. In the task of making disciples of our children, God empowers us by the Spirit, instructs us by the Scripture, equips us by the church, and uses our influence and authority that He gave to us in the parent-child relationship.

EMPOWERED BY THE SPIRIT OF GOD

We can make disciples of our children through the supernatural power of God's Spirit abiding in us. Jesus told us in John 15 that apart from Him we could never produce the fruit in our lives God expected of His followers. There, Jesus declared that He is the Vine and the Source of all things. We, on the other hand, are branches who are totally and desperately dependent upon Him. Jesus said we must abide in Him and He in us in order to produce the fruit that reflects the character and likeness of God. If we do not abide in Him, Jesus said we could do nothing to live out the life God redeemed for us to live.

Jesus did not say we would be slightly less able to do His work apart from Him. He did not say that we would produce a smaller amount of fruit if we lived by our own faculties. No, Jesus insisted that having a fruitful life and doing His work could not be produced apart from Him (Jn 15:5). God empowers us to live the life for which we were created. He divinely strengthens us to do the works He prepared for us. He invigorates us to accomplish the mission He established from the beginning. He does so in the person of the Holy Spirit. The Spirit of God indwells believers as God's temple or dwelling place, to give us, among other things, a supernatural strength to accomplish the work and will of God in our lives (1 Cor 3:16, Acts 7:48, 17:24).

Jesus directly spoke of the coming Spirit to dwell with believers toward the end of His earthly ministry. As He prepared His disciples for His departure, He spoke with them about His being delivered into the hands of the religious leaders who would crucify Him. He made known to them that a time would come when He would no longer be with them in flesh and blood. While this news grieved His disciples, Jesus reassured them that He would not leave them as orphans. He reminded them that He had come as their Helper to reconcile them to God through His death and resurrection. He then promised that the Holy Spirit would come as another Helper to be with them forever. The Spirit of God would teach them and guide them into all truth. Even more, He would dwell within them, enabling them to live as His disciples and to complete His mission of making disciples (Jn 14:16–18).

After His resurrection, Jesus spent forty days with His disciples. He taught them further and prepared them for the time of His departure. Then, gathering them together just moments before His ascension into heaven, He commanded them to wait in Jerusalem until the Holy Spirit came. Jesus constrained them not to set out in doing His work without first receiving the intended power for His work. Jesus knew that human ingenuity and natural strength are not enough to fulfill His mission. Good intentions and valiant human effort cannot suffice in making disciples. His mission requires supernatural power from above. Jesus revealed this to His followers when He told them first to receive His power by the Spirit before they began proclaiming the gospel, leading others to faith, teaching them to obey, and sending them out to reproduce other disciples (Acts 1:1–9). L. Nelson Bell writes, "No matter how high and holy one's aspirations the fact remains that the spirit may be willing but the flesh weak. There must come upon us a power which we do not already possess, a supernatural *Presence* who imparts and maintains within us supernatural power."[11]

---

[11] L. Nelson Bell, "A Layman and His Faith," *Christianity Today* (Washington, D.C.: Christianity Today, 1961), 281.

The disciples waited for ten days following Jesus' ascension. Waiting on God's promise is never easy though waiting is necessary. On the day of Pentecost, the disciples were gathered in a room together praying when the Spirit of God was poured out upon them. He gifted them with the ability to speak languages they had not previously learned so that the death and resurrection of Jesus could be proclaimed (Acts 2:1–4). They were able to declare the gospel, lead others to faith in Christ, and teach them to obey the commands of Jesus. They were able to do all this because God empowered them for the task on the day of Pentecost. But God enabled them to make disciples in the power of the His Spirit not just on the day of Pentecost along, but every other day as well.

The same Spirit who empowered Jesus' ministry, as well as that of the Apostles', dwells in believers today. He resides with God's people to empower us to advance His mission. John Stott writes, "Just as the Spirit came upon Jesus to equip him for his public ministry, so now the Spirit [comes] upon his people to equip them for theirs.[12]

Christian parents can rest confidently in the fact God has given His Spirit to them to supernaturally enable them to make disciples of their children. Like the many Christians making disciples throughout the pages of the New Testament, believing

[12] John R. W. Stott, *The Message of Acts: The Spirit, the Church & the World*, The Bible Speaks Today (Leicester, England; Downers Grove, IL: InterVarsity Press, 1994), 38–39.

parents are able by God's power to do the same. No follower of Jesus in the New Testament, including the Apostles, received a power to make disciples other than the Spirit of God. We can advance the gospel and make disciples of our children through the Spirit's power present and at work in our lives.

The Book of Acts reveals a number of ways God's Spirit enabled Jesus' followers to carry out the mission. The Spirit of God gave believers boldness to speak the gospel (Acts 2:4, 14). The Spirit provided wisdom to direct them in what to do in difficult circumstances (Acts 5:1–11). He imparted courage to them in the face of suffering and danger (Acts 7:54–60). He offered direction to them as to where He desired to place them in serving as part of His mission (Acts 8:26–40). He sustained passion and strength in them to continue in the work even when they were assaulted with hardship or plagued with uncertainty (Acts 20:22–23). What is unmistakable is the role of the Spirit of God to propel the Church forward through the ages. By giving us His Spirit, God has given us a power outside of our natural strength to fulfill His mission to make disciples. His power inside of us supersedes any power outside of us, including the collective power of all those in opposition to Jesus and His work (1 Jn 4:4).

INSTRUCTED BY THE SCRIPTURE

A second essential resource God has given His followers in making disciples is Scripture. God penned His Word through human agents upon whom the Spirit of God moved (2 Tim 3:16, 2 Pet 1:19–21).[13] Scripture stands apart from all other written literature as the divine declaration of the only wise, true, and immortal God (Rom 16:27, 1 Tim 1:17). The Bible is not merely the thoughts of mortal men, but a self-revelation of God to human beings. Gleason Archer writes, "When the Scripture speaks, it is God who speaks…"[14] Every time we read or hear the word of God, we hear the voice of God communicating to us His heart, mind, and will. No matter the time, the place, or the people, Scripture is the enduring word of God that will never change or pass away (Is 40:8).

God has given us His written words in order that we may know who He is, what He has done, who we are, and how we can live in a right, restored relationship with Him for His glory.[15] The Scripture is for both our *faith* and *practice*. He gave His Word to teach us the way to salvation. He also gave us Scripture to teach us the way to walk in the salvation we have received. The Bible teaches believers how "to live self-

---

[13] Kevin J. Vanhoozer, "Scripture, Doctrine Of," ed. Martin Davie et al., *New Dictionary of Theology: Historical and Systematic* (London; Downers Grove, IL: Inter-Varsity Press; InterVarsity Press, 2016), 828.

[14] Gleason Archer, *A Survey of Old Testament Introduction* (Chicago, Ill.: Moody Publishers, 2007), 31.

[15] David S. Dockery, "Scripture," ed. Chad Brand et al., *Holman Illustrated Bible Dictionary* (Nashville, TN: Holman Bible Publishers, 2003), 1453.

controlled, upright, and godly lives in the present age" (Titus 2:12). In Paul's second letter to Timothy, he reminded Timothy that Scripture has a divine origin and that God's Word provides practical guidance. Paul noted that God's Word teaches, corrects, rebukes, and trains us in righteousness so that we as His followers "may be complete, equipped for every good work" (2 Tim 3:16–17). Paul highlights that "scripture is given to enable any 'person of God' to meet the demands that God places on that person..."[16]

Disciples of Jesus can live out the demands of God in their particular calling, role, and responsibility because the Word of God offers the necessary instruction and teaching for how to live in obedience to God in that area of their lives. Never is there a deficiency in what the Bible gives us. We have been given "all the treasures of wisdom and knowledge" (Col 2:3). Therefore, as followers of Jesus who have received God's Spirit and His Word, we possess "everything we need for a godly life through our knowledge of him who called us by his own glory and goodness" (2 Pet 1:3).

That God has given us Scripture to provide us with all we need to be faithful to His calling on our lives should encourage parents as disciple-makers of the children. Parents find encouragement by first knowing that the Word of God is able to

---

[16] George W. Knight, *The Pastoral Epistles: A Commentary on the Greek Text*, New International Greek Testament Commentary (Grand Rapids, MI; Carlisle, England: W.B. Eerdmans; Paternoster Press, 1992), 450.

make all people wise unto salvation (2 Tim 3:15). Through the faithful reading and teaching of God's Word, individuals come to see their need for salvation and that Jesus Christ alone is the way of salvation.

Second, parents are encouraged in their spiritual work with their children by seeing that God's Word outlines for parents and children what God teaches in regard to living a holy and righteous life. The Scripture is the revelation of God that parents are to teach so that our children know God's commands. Even teaching our unbelieving children the Bible aids in bringing them to understand the seriousness of their disobedience to God and their weakness to meet God's righteous standard on their own. We teach them the truth of the Bible that points them to salvation through faith in the Person and work of Jesus Christ. In teaching our Christian children what God's Word teaches, they are able to know how to live worthy of Christ and His gospel that saved them to live in a relationship of worship and obedience to Him (Phil 1:27).

Third, although God did not pen Scripture as a parenting manual, throughout the Bible, God communicates His plan for the family. The family factors largely in the mission of God to make disciples. God purposed for the family to be at the heart of His mission to pass faith to successive generations. Therefore, God teaches and equips each individual of the family, by His Spirit and through His Word, to know and fulfill his or her God-given role and responsibility in the family, the Church, and the world. Scripture outlines not only the role God has given us, but the Bible also dictates how we are to faithfully live out our role. God addresses the family role and responsibility of husbands, wives, grandparents, parents, and children in His Word. There is no ambiguity in Scripture regarding what God's role is for parents and children and the relationship He intended between the two. In Scripture, God informs us as to what we are to teach, when we are to teach, and how we are to teach as parents (Deut 6:1–9, Ps 78:1–7; Matt 28:16–20, Col 1:28, 2 Tim 2:1–2).[17] Likewise, God calls upon children to submit to their parents' authority by listening and obeying their instructions, especially the divine injunctions from God's Word (Eph 6:1, Prov 1:8). God speaks commands to the family and each member of the family in particular. We need the essential teaching and wisdom of the Word of God to

---

[17] James Estep, Michael Anthony, Greg Allison, *A Theology for Christian Education* (Nashville, TN: B&H Publishing, 2008), 124–146. This particular work raises some serious concerns for the author. Namely, Estep, Anthony, and Allison state throughout that the Bible provides the content or theology of our teaching, while the social sciences should be consulted for our methodology. This is rather peculiar given the particular focus in the chapter entitled "Christology and Christian Education" that examines the methods employed by Jesus in His teaching ministry as recorded by the New Testament writers. Estep's chapter examining the various methods Jesus utilized in His teaching highlights the point that Scripture is for both *faith* and *practice*, though he denies this elsewhere in the book. Scripture declares that we are to teach and also instruct us in how we are to teach. Parents can examine the methods used by Jesus, as well as Peter, Paul, and others, as they embrace their role to teach their children and lead them be disciples of Jesus Christ. We may glean from doing so, as Estep notes, how Jesus taught using questions, parables, teachable moments, confrontation, and using Scripture as His material, which we, as parents, can utilize in teaching our children.

guide us in our endeavor of being and making lifetime disciples of Jesus Christ.

EQUIPPED BY THE LOCAL CHURCH

A third essential resource God has given to parents as disciple-makers of their children is the local church. God uses His church to equip His people, by His Spirit and through His Word, to carry out their calling and responsibility. God formed the church to be a people in relationship with Him. He also intends the church to co-labor with Him in fulfilling His mission of making disciples in the world. God uses the local church to equip each member to fulfill his or her calling, role, and responsibility in the family, the church, and the world.

THE CHURCH IS A FAMILY

The church is not simply an organization of people, but rather a family God has assembled together in Jesus Christ. All people were created to live in community with God and one another.[18] Sin, however, severed humanity's vertical relationship with God and shattered humanity's horizontal relationship to one another. These two relationships were given to humanity in which we were to live and flourish. Yet, sin brought a rift in both. When Christ came to die on the cross, in our place, for our sin, He aimed to bring His created image bearers back into

---

[18] Brad House, *Community* (Wheaton, Ill.: Crossway, 201), 32.

relationship with Himself and one another. By faith in the cross of Christ, the power of sin is broken, hearts are changed, and relationships restored. John Stott writes:

> [Sin] pulls people out of harmony with neighbors. It estranges them not only from their Maker but from their fellow-creatures. God's purpose has been to overthrow through Christ all the vile consequences of sin. His plan, therefore, is not to call independent, unconnected individuals to return to Himself in isolation from one another, but to redeem a people for His own possession.[19]

Salvation restores humanity into community with Him and one another that He intended for us to enjoy from the beginning of His creation. The death and resurrection of Jesus formed a new family, the church, from individuals who come to faith in Jesus Christ. Those who trust in Him for salvation are adopted as sons and daughters of the heavenly Father and made part of the household of God (Heb 2:10, Jn 1:12, Eph 2:19, Matt 6:9). Thus, the church paints a beautiful picture of the life-transforming power of the gospel that brings people once divided by sin into a peaceful, reconciled, and Christ-centered relationship with one another. The church is a family of sons and daughters returned into relationship with their heavenly father and one another. We are brothers and sisters in the family of God because of the reconciling work of Christ to unite us in relationship in God's family.

---

[19] John Stott, *Basic Christianity* (Chicago, IL: Inter-Varsity Press, 1964), 105.

THE CHURCH IS THE BODY OF CHRIST

As the family of God united under Jesus Christ, we are unified together as one. In addition to using the imagery of a household or family, Paul explained the new relationship of believers to Christ and one another using the metaphor of a unified body. The Head of the body is Jesus Christ (Col 1:28) and believers are the individual members or parts of the body (1 Cor 12). Jesus, as the Head, has absolute authority over His body. Individual members of the body are to submit to the authority of Jesus Christ first and foremost. Scripture teaches that Christ places members in the body as He sees fit. He also supplies to each member what he or she needs to function as part of the body. God gives a gift of grace to be used in service to Him and the body. A person who trusts in Jesus Christ receives a spiritual gift that God intends the believer to deploy in service to Him and the other members of His body (1 Cor 12:4–31, 1 Pet 4:10–11). Francis Foulkes pens, "The church is increased and built up, and its members edified, as each member uses his or her particular gifts as the Lord of the church ordains, and thus gives spiritual service to fellow-members and to the head."[20]

When believers live in community with one other and exercise their gifts in service to Christ and one another, the members of the church are built up in unity, faith, and spiritual

---

[20] Francis Foulkes, *Ephesians: An Introduction and Commentary*, vol. 10, Tyndale New Testament Commentaries (Downers Grove, IL: InterVarsity Press, 1989), 127.

maturity (Eph 4:12–13).[21] Not all believers have the same gift and no one person possesses all the spiritual gifts. When each person uses his or her gift within the body, the body functions together as it should and the other members experience growth, encouragement, and necessary training to fulfill their God-given calling and responsibility in the home, the church, and the world. All the spiritual gifts God gives to the various members of His body are necessary and needful. However, God emphasizes the importance of those gifted to preach and teach the truth of God as a means to instruct God's people in how to know and follow Jesus Christ through proper application of God's Word to their lives. This includes teachers and pastors (Js 3:1, Eph 4:11) as well as mature believers who instruct by precept and example in how to live as Christ followers (Titus 2:1–9).

Every disciple of Jesus Christ has specific roles and responsibilities to fulfill in the family, in the church, and in the world. These cannot be adequately carried out unless we are equipped for that role and its assignments. In regard to the family, there are the roles of husbands, wives, grandparents, fathers, mothers, and children. God has given the church as a community to equip these individuals to fulfill their roles. The body of Christ does so, in part, through scriptural teaching, godly example, faithful accountability, and intercessory prayer.

---

[21] John Stott, *God's New Society: The Message of Ephesians*, The Bible Speaks Today (Downers Grove, IL: InterVarsity Press, 1979), 168.

For fathers and mothers tasked with the primary role of seeing their children, who are alienated from God, reconciled through faith in Jesus Christ and His death and resurrection (2 Cor 5:11–21), God intended the corporate body of the church to equip them for this role and task. Parents need the church to faithfully call them to embrace their role, teach them how to diligently fulfill their role, pray for and encourage them as they undertake this role, and provide gracious, consistent accountability to obey Christ in meeting the expectations of God in their role and responsibility.

When parents fulfill their role and responsibility of leading their children to be disciples of Jesus, they serve Christ, their family, their church, and their children. By focusing on their children coming to faith in Jesus and growing in Christ-like maturity as His disciples, parents build godly homes, strong churches, and a better world as they increase the number of worshipping, obedient followers of Jesus on the earth who live life to love God and others. Thus, when the church equips parents to faithfully engage in their duty of making disciples of their children, the church benefits themselves and the world. Abraham Kuyper expresses this well when he writes, "The greatest gift a church can receive is to have a group of families who take their responsibilities with such Christian seriousness that they are willing to completely alter their lifestyle to raise up disciples for Jesus Christ."[22] When parents do this, the disciples they raise up establish godly homes and join the community of God's people in serving and equipping one another to have kingdom impact in this world.

THE CHURCH IS NOT A SUBSTITUTE

God meant for the church to equip parents continually for the mission of making disciples of their children and to send them home to commence this work daily. Tragically, the church often fails to equip parents, send them to be spiritual leaders at home, or hold them accountable as to whether they are obeying Jesus Christ in doing what He called them to do. Equally tragic is the fact that many parents believe sending their children to church once or twice a week suffices as an acceptable substitute for their own disciple-making efforts in the home.

Giving financially to the church so that the corporate body provides programming, staffing, and gathering space for our children must never be seen as supplying a sufficient substitute to make our children into disciples of Jesus Christ. Voddie Bauchum contends that parents' practice of sending their children to the local church in order to receive what God intended for parents to provide in the home stands as the reason so many children raised in homes with Christian parents are falling away from the faith. He argues that parents have inverted

---

[22] Kevin Swanson, "Corporate World to Hotdog Stand – Living God's Priorities and Values," *OnePlace*, October 30, 2017, accessed November 12, 2019: https://www.oneplace.com/ministries/generations-radio/listen/corporate-world-to-hot-dog-stand-living-gods-priorities-and-values-627186.html.

what God intended. He writes, "Our children are not falling away because the church is doing a poor job. Our children are falling away because we are asking the church to do what God designed the family to accomplish."[23] Bauchum then challenges, "At best, the church is to play a supporting role as it 'equips the saints for the work of ministry' (Ephesians 4:12, ESV)."[24] Parents are missionaries in their homes where they are expected to be ambassadors of Jesus Christ who make disciples of their children by leading them to faith in Jesus Christ and to mature as His followers in greater worship and obedience. The church must equip parents for this primary work of ministry and mission. Churches that fail to equip parents are a detriment to families, as well as the church, because their failure weakens both the earthly and spiritual family. Even more, churches that do not equip parents to be disciple-makers do a disservice to the world and those for whom we are to be ambassadors of God, leading them to be reconciled to Christ through the gospel.

POSITIONED WITH AUTHORITY AND INFLUENCE

A fourth and final resource God has given parents in their spiritual task of making disciples of their children is the authority and influence God gave to parents in their relationship with their children. God created the parent-child relationship

---

[23] Voddie Bauchum, *Family Driven Faith* (Wheaton, IL: Crossway, 2007), 9.

[24] Ibid.

with an authority and influence unmatched in any other relationship our children may have. While parents may place their children under the authority of others at times, and while others can and do exert some influence upon our children, no one else exceeds the God-given authority and influence of parents in the lives of their children.[25] The words and actions of parents influence greatly the moral and spiritual shape of their children.

God established the authority and influence of parents in the beginning. He gave parents authority in leading their children and teaching them God's commands. Parents have responsibility for the mental, emotional, physical, and spiritual well being of their children. No one else was to be delegated the primary oversight and authority of parents to their children. God gave this authority to parents that children are to respect as established by God. Children are to give honor and respect to their parents and obey their instructions. In addition to a place of authority, parents wield an influence upon their children.

We influence our children through the power of teaching and example. By words and actions, parents lay the foundation for how children will see and interact with the world. Parents

---

[25] Christian Smith and Melinda Denton, *Soul Searching* (New York, NY: Oxford University Press, 2005). Researchers Christian Smith and Melinda Denton conducted extensive research on the faith of young people in America. Based on their research their team concluded, "Contrary to popular misguided cultural stereotypes and frequent parental misconceptions, we believe that the evidence clearly shows that the single most important social influence on the religious and spiritual lives of adolescents is their parents" (p. 261).

are constantly communicating the answer by their word and example to the ultimate questions of our existence. These questions include: who are we, why are we, where are we, what has gone wrong, and what is the solution.[26] Every parent communicates to his or her children the answer to these ultimate questions, whether knowingly or unknowingly. Some do so in harmony with the Scripture, while others do so in contradiction to it. Children, even from their youngest years, desire to understand the answer to life's most important questions. They look primarily to their parents for understanding on these matters in both the instruction their parents give and the example displayed from their parents' lives.

The parents who are wise and godly provide teaching and live out the commands from God's Word. Children, who witness their parents' faith "vibrantly practiced—even imperfectly," tend to "remain serious Christians" as they grow and mature. These children still "sometimes go through bumpy spots in the road." However, parents who seek to follow Jesus Christ in belief and practice leads, in most cases, to their children remaining faithful as followers of Jesus.[27] That is because God designed parents as the primary spiritual

---

[26]Christopher Wright, *The Mission of God* (Downers Grove, Ill.: InterVarsity Press, 2006), 55.

[27] Glenn Stanton and Andrew Hess, "Millennial Faith Participation and Retention," n.p. Focus on the Family, August 2013, accessed 21 October 2016: http://media.focusonthefamily.com/fotf/pdf/about-us/focus-findings/millenial-faith-retention.pdf#_ga=1.132875596.392784255.1440477650.

authorities of their children who exert primary influence when it comes to the spiritual formation of their children's lives. Parents ought never to give away that which God has given to them. They should never concede the place of spiritual authority and influence to others that God has entrusted to them.

INFLUENCE VS. DETERMINE

When discussing the place of parents' spiritual authority and influence in the lives of their children, we must be cautious not to equate parents' influence and authority with the ability of parents to determine their children's faith. Kenda Creasy Dean makes this point, saying, "Research is nearly unanimous on this point: parents matter most in shaping the religious lives of their children. This is not to say that parents determine their children's spiritual destinies."[28] Scripture reminds us that parents cannot determine their children's faith or force their children's obedience to God. Numerous heartbreaking instances are recorded in the Bible where imperfect, yet godly, parents had rebellious children who did not worship or obey God. In every instance, the child made a personal, act of the will decision to reject God's authority. On the other hand, we find instances where children did not have godly upbringing but responded in faith to follow God.[29] Each case highlights that

---

[28] Kenda Creasy Dean, *Almost Christian* (New York, N.Y.; Oxford University Press, 2010), 112.

[29] In Genesis 4, Abel worshipped and obeyed God, having followed the

parents cannot determine, either good or ill, whether their children follow Jesus Christ or not. Parents do not *determine* their children's faith but they do bear significant *influence* on their children following Jesus Christ. Simply stated, the children of parents who walk in genuine faith and obedience to Jesus Christ are more likely to be followers of Jesus themselves. Children are impressionable and the path they are shepherded to follow often becomes the path they travel.

AUTHORITY AND INFLUENCE EXEMPLIFIED

Scripture provides notable examples of parents and grandparents who shepherded their children and grandchildren to live in a relationship of worship and obedience with God through faith in Jesus Christ. The New Testament introduces us to one example in Lois and Eunice. This mother and grandmother team leveraged the authority and influence of their

---

teaching and instruction passed to him by his Adam and Eve. Cain, his brother, received the same instruction. Yet he disregarded the teaching. As a result, he found that God would not accept his offering. In anger, he rose up in the field and killed Abel. Both sons received the same instruction from godly, though definitely imperfect, parents. Samuel honored God and obeyed His commands throughout his life and ministry. As he aged, the elders of Israel rejected the sons of Samuel because of their corruption that stood in clear contrast to the upright and blameless life of Samuel (1 Sam 8).

We also find individuals in Scripture, who in spite of the negative, ungodly influence of their parents in their lives, ended up walking in faith after God. Such was Josiah whom we read about in 2 Kings 21-22. Though his father Amon and grandfather Manasseh were both wicked and evil kings, Josiah did not follow in the path that they chose. We read that Josiah "did what was right in the eyes of the Lord and walked in all the way of David his father, and he did not turn aside to the right or to the left" (2 Kings 22:2).

God-given roles to lead Timothy to surrender his life to follow Jesus.

When Paul wrote his second letter to Timothy, he mentions the genuine faith of Timothy's grandmother, Lois, and mother, Eunice (2 Tim 1:5). The conspicuous omission of Timothy's father here is likely because his father was a Gentile unbeliever (Acts 16:1). Despite the unbelief of his father, Paul notes that Timothy possessed a sincere faith in Jesus Christ that first existed in his mother and grandmother. Lois and Eunice did not force Timothy to faith in Jesus Christ, for that they could not do. They did not choose for Timothy to be a disciple of Jesus, for again that was outside their ability and authority. What they did was exercise faithful and loving influence from their positions of God-given authority in Timothy's life. They did so by teaching him the Scriptures and pointing him to trust in Jesus Christ as Savior and Lord. They directed Timothy to believe God's Word, trust in God for salvation, and live a life of honor to God through obedience and worship (2 Tim 3:15–16). John Stott pens, "True, no man can inherit his parents' faith in the way that he inherits facets of their personality. But a child can be led to faith by his parents' teaching, example and prayers."[30] Such was the case with Timothy. He came to faith because of

---

[30] John Stott, *Guard the Gospel the Message of 2 Timothy*, The Bible Speaks Today (Downers Grove, IL: InterVarsity Press, 1973), 27. See also Knute Larson, "I & II Thessalonians, I & II Timothy, Titus, Philemon," in *Holman New Testament Commentary*, vol. 9 (Nashville, TN: Broadman & Holman Publishers, 2000), 265.

the persistence of his grandmother and mother. They not only imparted the truth to Him, but they personified truth in practice.

Lois and Eunice demonstrate the influence grandparents and parents can have on the next generation when it comes to their faith and followership of Jesus Christ. Parents have been bestowed a position of authority and influence with their children to be utilized most for making disciples. Through the power of the Spirit, the instruction of Scripture, and the equipping by the local church, God can use parents in their relationship with their kids to bring up a generation of faithful disciples of Jesus Christ.

NOW WHAT?

Our journey across these three chapters established that all people were made to live in a relationship of worship and obedience as followers of God through Jesus Christ. God designed the parent-child relationship specifically to accomplish this kingdom purpose. Though humanity's rebellion separates men and women from God, God's heart has never changed toward us. God pursues us for relationship that we may be His people who delight in Him and He in us. He reconciles us into relationship with Himself through Jesus' death and resurrection by delivering us from sin and its consequences of death, destruction, and eternal separation from Him. Jesus Christ died and rose again to pardon our offense of sin and bridge the chasm between God and us carved out by our rebellion. Jesus Christ stands as the only way for sinful human beings to be restored to relationship with God. Through Him we are to live in a relationship of worship and obedience with Him forever.

Christian parents bear the primary responsibility of leading their children back into relationship with God through Jesus Christ. Parents are to help their children to hear and see the gospel in their home. They are to lead their children to place their faith in Jesus Christ. Parents are to instruct their children to walk in obedience to Jesus' teaching and engage in His mission. To fulfill this task, God has given to parents His Spirit, His Word, His Church, and the authority and influence of the parent-child relationship.

Yet here is the crux of the matter: We can know truth and yet not live the truth. Right belief does not always manifest in right practice. For sure, we cannot live rightly if we do not believe rightly. But knowledge of what is true is of no use unless it is acted upon in faith and obedience. Knowing this, James wrote to first-century Christians who apparently wrestled with knowing the truth but not living it out. He challenged them not to be hearers of the truth but to be practitioners of the truth (Js 1:22). As it relates to parents, this simply means we can know we have primary responsibility for the spiritual leadership of our children and their faith formation, yet fail to engage in the task of making disciples of our children.

We dare not ignore the work, minimize the importance of the task, or seek to place the duty of making disciples of our children upon someone else. So the question we must ask of ourselves is this: What will we choose? Will we—parents, primarily, as well as grandparents—seek to be faithful and obedient in God's mission of making disciples of our children, grandchildren, and the next generation? God will hold us accountable for our decision. He will examine each of our lives in the end to judge us as to whether we engaged in the work of making disciples of the ones He entrusted to us.

J. C. Ryle's words that follow offer practical and helpful direction for parents in this endeavor. His instructions and the practical truth he shares, however, have no weight or benefit if we do not commit to practice what we hear and learn. Will you trust God's plan for making disciples of your children? Will you surrender yourself into God's hands as the chief instrument He made for leading your children to know and follow Him? Will you use the resources He has provided to supply all you need in this endeavor?

Before you move further into the next section, would you pause to enter the presence of God through prayer to surrender yourself to fulfill His mission? Will you take time to give your children as an offering to God for His will and service? Would you take a moment to petition God for what you need to faithfully carry out your responsibility in making disciples? The following prayer from Andrew Murray may be helpful in directing your heart and prayer to God.

A PARENT'S PRAYER

"Gracious and most blessed Father, I bow before You once again that I may fully comprehend Your holy purpose with an earthly parentage, to transmit through it Your blessing. O my God, let Your word, *my salvation from generation to generation*, so fill my heart that my calling and duty with Your promise and purpose may be equally clear to me, and the salvation of my children be as sure as my own.

And grant, Lord, that in Your light I may realize and manifest fully what salvation is—salvation from sin and its power unto the holiness and the service of God. Let it be in me a salvation that fills my heart with gladness and my lips with praise and my whole life with purity and love. Let the salvation in which I walk and in which I train the children be the salvation of God.

O my God, I ask You, give me grace as the one heirloom my children cherish in their parents, the one thing transmitted in our home from child to child, the salvation, the love, the joy, the service to God. Yes, Lord, You are the Eternal and Unchanging One; let it be from generation to generation. Amen."[31]

---

[31] Murray, *How to Raise Children for Christ*, 127–128.

CHAPTER 4

THE DUTIES OF PARENTS

*"Train up a child in the way he should go;
and when he is old, he will not depart from it."*

Proverbs 22:6

I SUPPOSE that most professing Christians are acquainted with the text at the head of this page. The sound of it is probably familiar to your ears, like an old tune. It is likely you have heard it, or read it, talked of it, or quoted it, many a time. Is it not so?

But, after all, how little is the substance of this text regarded! The doctrine it contains appears scarcely known, the duty it puts before us seems fearfully seldom practiced. Reader, do I not speak the truth?

It cannot be said that the subject is a new one. The world is old, and we have the experience of nearly six thousand years to help us. We live in days when there is a mighty zeal for education in every quarter. We hear of new schools rising on all sides. We are told of new systems and new books for the young, of every sort and description. And still for all this, the vast majority of children are manifestly not trained in the way they should go, for when they grow up to man's estate, they do not walk with God.

Now how shall we account for this state of things? The plain truth is the Lord's commandment in our text is not regarded; and therefore the Lord's promise in our text is not fulfilled.

Reader, these things may well give rise to great searchings of heart. Suffer then a word of exhortation from a minister about the right training of children. Believe me, the subject is one that should come home to every conscience, and make every one ask himself the question, "Am I in this matter doing what I can?" It is a subject that concerns almost all. There is hardly a household that it does not touch. Parents, nurses, teachers, godfathers, godmothers, uncles, aunts, brothers, sisters all have an interest in it. Few can be found, I think, who might not influence some parent in the management of his family, or affect the training of some child by suggestion or advice. All of us, I suspect, can do something here, either directly or indirectly, and I wish to stir up all to bear this in remembrance.

It is a subject, too, on which all concerned are in great danger of coming short of their duty. This is preeminently a point in which men can see the faults of their neighbors more clearly than their own. They will often bring up their children in the very path, which they have denounced to their friends as unsafe. They will see motes in other men's families, and overlook beams in their own. They will be quick sighted as eagles in detecting mistakes abroad, and yet blind as bats to fatal errors, which are daily going on at home. They will be wise about their brother's house, but foolish about their own flesh and blood. Here, if anywhere, we have need to suspect our own judgment. This, too, you will do well to bear in mind.

As a minister, I cannot help remarking that there is hardly any subject about which people seem so tenacious as they are about their children. I have sometimes been perfectly astonished at the slowness of sensible Christian parents to allow that their own children are in fault or deserve blame. There are not a few persons to whom I would far rather speak about their own sins than tell them their children had done anything wrong.

Come now and let me place before you a few hints about right training. God the Father, God the Son, God the Holy Spirit bless them, and make them words in season to you all. Reject them not because they are blunt and simple; despise them not because they contain nothing new. Be very sure, if you would train children for heaven, they are hints that ought not to be lightly set aside.

CHAPTER 5

TRAIN THEM IN THE WAY THEY SHOULD GO, AND NOT IN THE WAY THAT THEY WOULD

Remember children are born with a decided bias towards evil and, therefore, if you let them choose for themselves, they are certain to choose wrong.

The mother cannot tell what her tender infant may grow up to be, tall or short, weak or strong, wise or foolish. He may be any of these things or not; it is all uncertain. But one thing the mother can say with certainty: he will have a corrupt and sinful heart. It is natural to us to do wrong. "Foolishness," says Solomon, "is bound in the heart of a child" (Prov 22:15). "A child left to himself brings his mother to shame" (Prov 24:15). Our hearts are like the earth on which we tread; let it alone and it is sure to bear weeds.

If, then, you would deal wisely with your child, you must not leave him to the guidance of his own will. Think for him, judge for him, act for him, just as you would for one weak and blind; but for pity's sake, give him not up to his own wayward tastes and inclinations. It must not be his likings and wishes that are consulted. He knows not yet what is good for his mind and soul any more than what is good for his body. You do not let him decide what he shall eat, what he shall drink, and how he shall be clothed. Be consistent, and deal with his mind in like manner. Train him in the way that is scriptural and right and not in the way that he fancies.

If you cannot make up your mind to this first principle of Christian training, it is useless for you to read any further. Self-will is almost the first thing that appears in a child's mind; and it must be your first step to resist it.

CHAPTER 6

TRAIN UP YOUR CHILD WITH ALL TENDERNESS, AFFECTION, AND PATIENCE

I do not mean that you are to spoil him, but I do mean that you should let him see that you love him.

Love should be the silver thread that runs through all your conduct. Kindness, gentleness, long-suffering, forbearance, patience, sympathy, a willingness to enter into childish troubles, a readiness to take part in childish joys, these are the cords by which a child may be led most easily. These are the clues you must follow if you would find the way to his heart.

Few are to be found, even among grown-up people, who are not easier to draw than to drive. There is that in all our minds which rises in arms against compulsion. We set up our backs and stiffen our necks at the very idea of a forced obedience. We are like young horses in the hand of a breaker: handle them kindly, make much of them, and by and by you may guide them with thread. Use them roughly and violently and it will be many a month before you get the mastery of them at all.

Now children's minds are cast in much the same mold as our own. Sternness and severity of manner chill them and throw them back. It shuts up their hearts and you will weary yourself to find the door. But let them only see that you have an affectionate feeling towards them, that you are really desirous to make them happy and do them good. That if you punish them, it is intended for their profit, and that, like the pelican, you would give your heart's blood to nourish their souls. Let them see this, I say, and they will soon be all your own. But they must be wooed with kindness if their attention is ever to be won.

And surely reason itself might teach us this lesson. Children are weak and tender creatures, and, as such, they need patient and considerate treatment. We must handle them delicately, like frail machines, lest by rough fingering we do more harm than good. They are like young plants and need gentle watering, often, but little at a time.

We must not expect all things at once. We must remember what children are and teach them as they are able to bear. Their minds are like a lump of metal not to be forged and made useful at once, but only by a succession of little blows. Their understandings are like narrow-necked vessels: we must pour in the wine of knowledge gradually or much of it will be spilled and lost. "Line upon line, and precept upon precept, here a little and there a little," must be our rule. The whetstone does its work slowly, but frequent rubbing will bring the scythe to a fine edge. Truly there is need of patience in training a child, but without it nothing can be done.

Nothing will compensate for the absence of this tenderness and love. A minister may speak the truth as it is in Jesus, clearly, forcibly, and unanswerably. But if he does not speak it in love, few souls will be won. Likewise, you must set before your children their duty, command, threaten, punish, reason, but if affection be wanting in your treatment, your labor will be all in vain.

Love is one grand secret of successful training. Anger and harshness may frighten, but they will not persuade the child that you are right; and if he sees you often out of temper, you will soon cease to have his respect. A father who speaks to his son as Saul did to Jonathan (1 Sam 20:30), need not expect to retain his influence over that son's mind.

Try hard to keep up a hold on your child's affections. It is a dangerous thing to make your children afraid of you. Anything is almost better than reserve and constraint between your child and yourself; and this will come in with fear. Fear puts an end to openness of manner; fear leads to concealment; fear sows the seed of much hypocrisy, and leads to many a lie. There is a mine of truth in the Apostle's words to the Colossians: "Fathers, provoke not your children to anger, lest they be discouraged" (Col 3:21). Let not the advice it contains be overlooked.

CHAPTER 7

TRAIN YOUR CHILDREN WITH AN ABIDING PERSUASION ON YOUR MIND THAT MUCH DEPENDS UPON YOU

Grace is the strongest of all principles. See what a revolution grace effects when it comes into the heart of an old sinner; how it overturns the strongholds of Satan, how it casts down mountains, fills up valleys, makes crooked things straight, and new creates the whole man. Truly nothing is impossible to grace.

Nature, too, is very strong. See how it struggles against the things of the kingdom of God, how it fights against every attempt to be more holy, and how it keeps up an unceasing warfare within us to the last hour of life. Nature indeed is strong. But after nature and grace, undoubtedly, there is nothing more powerful than education. Early habits (if I may so speak) are everything with us under God. We are made what we are by training. Our character takes the form of that mold into which our first years are cast.

"He has seen but little of life who does not discern

everywhere the effect of education on men's opinions and habits of thinking. The children bring out of the nursery that which displays itself throughout their lives." *Richard Cecil.*

We depend, in a vast measure, on those who bring us up. We get from them a color, a taste, and a bias, which cling to us more or less all our lives. We catch the language of our nurses and mothers and learn to speak it almost insensibly and unquestionably. We catch something of their manners, ways, and mind at the same time. Time only will show, I suspect, how much we all owe to early impressions and how many things in us may be traced up to seeds sown in the days of our very infancy by those who were about us. A very learned Englishman, John Locke, has gone so far as to say: "That of all the men we meet with, nine parts out of ten are what they are, good or bad, useful or not, according to their education."

And all this is one of God's merciful arrangements. He gives your children a mind that will receive impressions like moist clay. He gives them a disposition at the starting-point of life to believe what you tell them, to take for granted what you advise them, and to trust your word rather than a stranger's. He gives you, in short, a golden opportunity of doing them good. See that the opportunity be not neglected and thrown away. Once let slip, it is gone forever.

Beware of that miserable delusion into which some have fallen, that parents can do nothing for their children, that you must leave them alone, wait for grace, and sit still. These persons have wishes for their children in Balaam's fashion. They would like them to die the death of the righteous man, but they do nothing to make them live his life. They desire much and have nothing. And the devil rejoices to see such reasoning, just as he always does over anything that seems to excuse indolence or to encourage neglect of means.

I know that you cannot convert your child. I know well that they who are born again are born, not of the will of man, but of God. But I know also that God says expressly, "Train up a child in the way he should go," and that He never laid a command on man which He would not give man grace to perform. And I know, too, that our duty is not to stand still and dispute, but to go forward and obey. It is just in the going forward that God will meet us. The path of obedience is the way in which He gives the blessing. We have only to do as the servants were commanded at the marriage feast in Cana, to fill the water-pots with water. We may safely leave it to the Lord to turn that water into wine.

CHAPTER 8

TRAIN WITH THIS THOUGHT CONTINUALLY BEFORE YOUR EYES THAT THE SOUL OF YOUR CHILD IS THE FIRST THING TO BE CONSIDERED

Precious, no doubt, are these little ones in your eyes. But if you love them, think often of their souls. No interest should weigh with you so much as their eternal interests. No part of them should be so dear to you as that part which will never die. The world, with all its glory, shall pass away. The hills shall melt, the heavens shall be wrapped together as a scroll, and the sun shall cease to shine. But the spirit that dwells in those little creatures, whom you love so well, shall outlive them all, and whether in happiness or misery (to speak as a man) will depend on you.

This is the thought that should be uppermost on your mind in all you do for your children. In every step you take about them, in every plan, and scheme, and arrangement that concerns them, do not leave out that mighty question, "How will this affect their souls?"

Soul love is the soul of all love. To pet and pamper and

indulge your child, as if this world was all he had to look to and this life the only season for happiness to do this, is not true love but cruelty. It is treating him like some beast of the earth, which has but one world to look to, and nothing after death. It is hiding from him that grand truth, which he ought to be made to learn from his very infancy, that the chief end of his life is the salvation of his soul.

A true Christian must be no slave to fashion, if he would train his child for heaven. He must not be content to do things merely because they are the custom of the world. To teach them and instruct them in certain ways, merely because it is usual; to allow them to read books of a questionable sort, merely because everybody else reads them; to let them form habits of a doubtful tendency, merely because they are the habits of the day. He must train with an eye to his children's souls. He must not be ashamed to hear his training called singular and strange. What if it is? The time is short. The fashion of this world passes away. He that has trained his children for heaven, rather than for earth, for God, rather than for man, he is the parent that will be called wise at last.

CHAPTER 9

TRAIN YOUR CHILD TO A
KNOWLEDGE OF THE BIBLE

You cannot make your children love the Bible, I allow. None but the Holy Spirit can give us a heart to delight in the Word. But you can make your children acquainted with the Bible. And be sure they cannot be acquainted with that blessed book too soon or too well. A thorough knowledge of the Bible is the foundation of all clear views of religion. He that is well grounded in it will not generally be found a waverer and carried about by every wind of new doctrine. Any system of training which does not make a knowledge of Scripture the first thing is unsafe and unsound.

You have need to be careful on this point just now, for the devil is abroad and error abounds. Some are to be found amongst us who give the Church the honor due to Jesus Christ. Some are to be found who make the sacraments saviors and passports to eternal life. And some are to be found in like manner who honor a catechism more than the Bible or fill the minds of their children with miserable little storybooks, instead of the Scripture of truth. But if you love your children, let the simple Bible be everything in the training of their souls; and let all other books go down and take the second place. Care not so much for their being mighty in the catechism, as for their being mighty in the Scriptures. This is the training, believe me, that God will honor. The Psalmist says of Him, "Thou hast magnified Thy Word above all Thy name" (Ps 138:2), and I think that He gives an especial blessing to all who try to magnify it among men.

See that your children read the Bible *reverently*. Train them to look on it, not as the word of men, but as it is in truth, the Word of God, written by the Holy Spirit Himself, all true, all profitable, and able to make us wise unto salvation, through faith which is in Christ Jesus.

See that they read it *regularly*. Train them to regard it as their soul's daily food, as a thing essential to their soul's daily health. I know well you cannot make this anything more than a form; but there is no telling the amount of sin which a mere form may indirectly restrain.

See that they read it *all*. You need not shrink from bringing any doctrine before them. You need not fancy that the leading doctrines of Christianity are things that children cannot understand. Children understand far more of the Bible than we are apt to suppose.

Tell them of sin, its guilt, its consequences, its power, and its vileness. You will find they can comprehend something of this.

Tell them of the Lord Jesus Christ, His work for our salvation, the atonement, the cross, the blood, the sacrifice, and the intercession. You will discover there is something not beyond them in all this.

Tell them of the work of the Holy Spirit in man's heart, how He changes, renews, sanctifies, and purifies. You will soon see they can go along with you in some measure in this. In short, I suspect we have no idea how much a little child can take in of the length and breadth of the glorious gospel. They see far more of these things than we suppose.

As to the age when the religious instruction of a child should begin, no general rule can be laid down. The mind seems to open in some children much more quickly than in others. We seldom begin too early. There are wonderful examples on record of what a child can attain to, even at three years old.

Fill their minds with Scripture. Let the Word dwell in them richly. Give them the Bible, the whole Bible, even while they are young.

CHAPTER 10

TRAIN THEM TO A HABIT OF PRAYER

Prayer is the very life-breath of true religion. It is one of the first evidences that a man is born again. "Behold," said the Lord of Saul, in the day he sent Ananias to him, "Behold, he prays" (Acts 9:11). He had begun to pray, and that was proof enough.

Prayer was the distinguishing mark of the Lord's people in the day that there began to be a separation between them and the world. "Then began men to call upon the name of the Lord" (Gen 4:26).

Prayer is the peculiarity of all real Christians now. They pray, for they tell God their wants, their feelings, their desires, their fears; and mean what they say. The nominal Christian may repeat prayers, and good prayers too, but he goes no further.

Prayer is the turning point in a man's soul. Our ministry is unprofitable, and our labor is vain, till you are brought to your knees. Till then, we have no hope about you.

Prayer is one great secret of spiritual prosperity. When there is much private communion with God, your soul will grow like the grass after rain. When there is little, all will be at a standstill; you will barely keep your soul alive. Show me a growing Christian, a going forward Christian, a strong Christian, a flourishing Christian, and sure am I, he is one that speaks often with his Lord. He asks much and he has much. He tells Jesus everything, and so he always knows how to act.

Prayer is the mightiest engine God has placed in our hands. It is the best weapon to use in every difficulty and the surest remedy in every trouble. It is the key that unlocks the treasury of promises, and the hand that draws forth grace and help in time of need. It is the silver trumpet God commands us to sound in all our necessity, and it is the cry He has promised always to attend to, even as a loving mother to the voice of her child.

Prayer is the simplest means that man can use in coming to God. It is within reach of all—the sick, the aged, the infirm, the paralytic, the blind, the poor, and the unlearned. All can pray. It avails you nothing to plead want of memory, want of learning, want of books, and want of scholarship in this matter. So long as you have a tongue to tell your soul's state, you may and ought to pray. Those words, "Ye have not, because ye ask not" (Jas 4:2), will be a fearful condemnation to many in the Day of Judgment.

Parents, if you love your children, do all that lies in your power to train them up to a habit of prayer. Show them how to begin. Tell them what to say. Encourage them to persevere. Remind them if they become careless and slack about it. Let it not be your fault, at any rate, if they never call on the name of the Lord.

This, remember, is the first step in religion which a child is able to take. Long before he can read, you can teach him to kneel by his mother's side, and repeat the simple words of prayer and praise which she puts in his mouth. And as the first steps in any undertaking are always the most important, so is the manner in which your children's prayers are prayed, a point that deserves your closest attention. Few seem to know how much depends on this. You must beware lest they get into a way of saying them in a hasty, careless, and irreverent manner. You must beware of giving up the oversight of this matter to servants and nurses, or of trusting too much to your children doing it when left to themselves. I cannot praise that mother who never looks after this most important part of her child's daily life herself. Surely if there be any habit which your own hand and eye should help in forming, it is the habit of prayer. Believe me, if you never hear your children pray yourself, you are much to blame. You are little wiser than the bird described in Job, "which leaves her eggs in the earth, and warms them in the dust, and forgets that the foot may crush them, or that the wild beast may break them. She is hardened against her young ones, as though they were not hers: her labor is in vain without fear" (Job 34:14–16).

Prayer is, of all habits, the one that we recollect the longest.

Many a grey-headed man could tell you how his mother used to make him pray in the days of his childhood. Other things have passed away from his mind perhaps. The church where he was taken to worship, the minister whom he heard preach, the companions who used to play with him, all these, it may be, have passed from his memory and left no mark behind. But you will often find it is far different with his first prayers. He will often be able to tell you where he knelt, what he was taught to say, and even how his mother looked all the while. It will come up as fresh before his mind's eye as if it was but yesterday.

Reader, if you love your children, I charge you, do not let the seedtime of a prayerful habit pass away unimproved. If you train your children to anything, train them, at least, to a habit of prayer.

CHAPTER 11

TRAIN THEM TO HABITS OF DILIGENCE AND REGULARITY ABOUT PUBLIC MEANS OF GRACE

Tell them of the duty and privilege of going to the house of God and joining in the prayers of the congregation. Tell them that wherever the Lord's people are gathered together, there the Lord Jesus is present in an especial manner, and that those who absent themselves must expect, like the Apostle Thomas, to miss a blessing. Tell them of the importance of hearing the Word preached, and that it is God's ordinance for converting, sanctifying, and building up the souls of men. Tell them how the Apostle Paul enjoins us not "to forsake the assembling of ourselves together, as the manner of some is" (Hebrews 10:25), but to exhort one another, to stir one another up to it, and so much the more as we see the day approaching.

I call it a sad sight in a church when nobody comes up to the Lord's Table but the elderly people, and the young men and the young women all turn away. But I call it a sadder sight still when no children are to be seen in a church, excepting those who come to the Sunday School and are obliged to attend. Let none of this guilt lie at your doors. There are many boys and girls in every parish, besides those who come to school, and you who are their parents and friends should see to it that they come with you to church.

Do not allow them to grow up with a habit of making vain excuses for not coming. Give them plainly to understand, that so long as they are under your roof it is the rule of your house for every one in health to honor the Lord's house upon the Lord's Day, and that you reckon the Sabbath-breaker to be a murderer of his own soul.

See to it too, if it can be so arranged, that your children go with you to church and sit near you when they are there. To go to church is one thing, but to behave well at church is quite another. And believe me, there is no security for good behavior like that of having them under your own eye.

The minds of young people are easily drawn aside and their attention lost, and every possible means should be used to counteract this. I do not like to see them coming to church by themselves. They often get into bad company by the way and so learn more evil on the Lord's Day than in all the rest of the week. Neither do I like to see what I call "a young people's corner" in a church. They often catch habits of inattention and irreverence there, which it takes years to unlearn, if ever they are unlearned at all. What I like to see is a whole family sitting together, old and young, side-by-side, men, women, and children, serving God according to their households.

But there are some who say that it is useless to urge children to attend means of grace because they cannot understand them.

I would not have you listen to such reasoning. I find no such doctrine in the Old Testament. When Moses goes before Pharaoh (Ex 10:9), I observe he says, "We will go with our young and with our old, with our sons and with our daughters: for we must hold a feast unto the Lord." When Joshua read the law (Josh 8:35), I observe, "There was not a word which Joshua read not before all the congregation of Israel, with the women and the little ones, and the strangers that were conversant among them." "Thrice in the year," says Exodus 34:23, "shall all your men children appear before the Lord God, the God of Israel." And when I turn to the New Testament, I find children mentioned there as partaking in public acts of religion as well as in the Old. When Paul was leaving the disciples at Tyre for the last time, I find it said (Acts 21:5), "They all brought us on our way, with wives and children, till we were out of the city: and we kneeled down on the shore, and prayed."

Samuel, in the days of his childhood, appears to have ministered unto the Lord some time before he really knew Him. "Samuel did not yet know the Lord, neither was the word of the Lord yet revealed unto him" (1 Sam 3:7). The Apostles themselves do not seem to have understood all that our Lord said at the time that it was spoken: "These things understood not His disciples at the first: but when Jesus was glorified, then remembered they that these things were written of Him" (Jn 12:16).

Parents, comfort your minds with these examples. Be not cast down because your children see not the full value of the means of grace now. Only train them up to a habit of regular attendance. Set it before their minds as a high, holy, and solemn duty, and, believe me, the day will very likely come when they will bless you for your deed.

CHAPTER 12

TRAIN THEM TO A HABIT OF FAITH

I mean by this, you should train them up to believe what you say. You should try to make them feel confidence in your judgment and respect your opinions, as better than their own. You should accustom them to think that, when you say a thing is bad for them, it must be bad, and when you say it is good for them, it must be good; that your knowledge, in short, is better than their own, and that they may rely implicitly on your word. Teach them to feel that what they know not now, they will probably know hereafter, and to be satisfied there is a reason and a needs-be for everything you require them to do.

Who indeed can describe the blessedness of a real spirit of faith? Or rather, who can tell the misery that unbelief has brought upon the world? Unbelief made Eve eat the forbidden fruit. She doubted the truth of God's word: "Ye shall surely die." Unbelief made the old world reject Noah's warning, and so perish in sin. Unbelief kept Israel in the wilderness. It was the bar that kept them from entering the Promised Land. Unbelief made the Jews crucify the Lord of glory; they believed not the voice of Moses and the prophets, though read to them every day. And unbelief is the reigning sin of man's heart down to this very hour, unbelief in God's promises, unbelief in God's threatenings, unbelief in our own sinfulness, unbelief in our own danger, and unbelief in everything that runs counter to the pride and worldliness of our evil hearts. Reader, you train your children to little purpose if you do not train them to a habit of implicit faith, faith in their parents' word, confidence that what their parents say must be right.

I have heard it said by some, that you should require nothing of children that they cannot understand; that you should explain and give a reason for everything you desire them to do. I warn you solemnly against such a notion. I tell you plainly, I think it an unsound and rotten principle. No doubt it is absurd to make a mystery of everything you do. There are many things that it is well to explain to children in order that they may see that they are reasonable and wise. But to bring them up with the idea that they must take nothing on trust, that they, with their weak and imperfect understandings, must have the "why" and the "wherefore" made clear to them at every step they take, this is indeed a fearful mistake and likely to have the worst effect on their minds.

Reason with your child if you are so disposed, at certain times, but never forget to keep him in mind (if you really love him) that he is but a child after all, that he thinks as a child, he understands as a child, and, therefore, must not expect to know the reason of everything at once.

Set before him the example of Isaac in the day when Abraham took him to offer him on Mount Moriah (Genesis 22). He asked his father that single question, "Where is the lamb for a burnt- offering?" and he got no answer but this, "God will provide Himself a lamb." How, or where, or whence, or in what manner, or by what means, all this Isaac was not told; but the answer was enough. He believed that it would be well, because his father said so and he was content.

Tell your children, too, that we must all be learners in our beginnings, that there is an alphabet to be mastered in every kind of knowledge, that the best horse in the world had need once to be broken, and that a day will come when they will see the wisdom of all your training. But in the meantime if you say a thing is right, it must be enough for them. They must believe you and be content.

Parents, if any point in training is important, it is this. I charge you by the affection you have to your children, use every means to train them up to a habit of faith.

CHAPTER 13

TRAIN THEM TO A HABIT OF OBEDIENCE

This is an object that it is worth any labor to attain. No habit, I suspect, has such an influence over our lives as this. Parents, determine to make your children obey you, though it may cost you much trouble and cost them many tears. Let there be no questioning, reasoning, disputing, delaying, and answering again. When you give them a command, let them see plainly that you will have it done.

Obedience is the only reality. It is faith visible, faith acting, and faith incarnate. It is the test of real discipleship among the Lord's people. "You are My friends if you do whatsoever I command you" (Jn 15:14). It ought to be the mark of well-trained children that they do whatsoever their parents command them. Where, in deed, is the honor that the fifth commandment enjoins, if fathers and mothers are not obeyed cheerfully, willingly, and at once?

Early obedience has all Scripture on its side. It is in Abraham's praise, not merely he will train his family, but "he will command his children, and his household after him" (Gen

18:19). It is said of the Lord Jesus Christ Himself that when "He was young He was subject to Mary and Joseph" (Luke 2:51). Observe how implicitly Joseph obeyed the order of his father Jacob (Gen 37:13). See how Isaiah speaks of it as an evil thing when "the child shall behave himself proudly against the ancient" (Is 3:5). Mark how the Apostle Paul names disobedience to parents as one of the bad signs of the latter days (2 Tim 3:2). Mark how he singles out this grace of requiring obedience as one that should adorn a Christian minister: "A bishop must be one that rules well his own house, having his children in subjection with all gravity." And again, "Let the deacons rule their children and their own houses well" (1 Tim 3:4,12). And again, an elder must be one "having faithful children, children not accused of riot, or unruly" (Titus 1:6).

Parents, do you wish to see your children happy? Take care, then, that you train them to obey when they are spoken to and to do as they are bid. Believe me, we are not made for entire independence. We are not fit for it. Even Christ's freemen have a yoke to wear; they "serve the Lord Christ" (Colossians 3:24). Children cannot learn too soon that this is a world in which we are not all intended to rule and that we are never in our right place until we know how to obey our betters. Teach them to obey while young or else they will be fretting against God all their lives long and wear themselves out with the vain idea of being independent of His control.

Reader, this hint is only too much needed. You will see many in this day who allow their children to choose and think for themselves long before they are able and even make excuses for their disobedience, as if it were a thing not to be blamed. To my eyes, a parent always yielding, and a child always having his or her own way, are a most painful sight. Painful because I see God's appointed order of things inverted and turned upside down. Painful because I feel sure the consequence to that child's character in the end will be self-will, pride, and self-conceit. You must not wonder that men refuse to obey their Father who is in heaven, if you allow them, when children, to disobey their father who is upon earth.

Parents, if you love your children, let obedience be a motto and a watchword continually before their eyes.

CHAPTER 14

TRAIN THEM TO A HABIT OF
ALWAYS SPEAKING THE TRUTH

Truth-speaking is far less common in the world than at first sight we are disposed to think. The whole truth, and nothing but the truth, is a golden rule which many would do well to bear in mind. Lying and prevarication are old sins. The devil was the father of them. He deceived Eve by a bold lie and ever since the fall it is a sin against which all the children of Eve have need to be on their guard.

Only think how much falsehood and deceit there is in the world! How much exaggeration! How many additions are made to a simple story! How many things left out, if it does not serve the speaker's interest to tell them! How few there are about us of whom we can say, we put unhesitating trust in their word! Verily the ancient Persians were wise in their generation. It was a leading point with them in educating their children that they should learn to speak the truth. What an awful proof it is of man's natural sinfulness that it should be needful to name such a point at all!

Reader, I would have you remark how often God is spoken of in the Old Testament as the God of truth. Truth seems to be especially set before us as a leading feature in the character of Him with whom we have to do. He never swerves from the straight line. He abhors lying and hypocrisy. Try to keep this continually before your children's minds. Press upon them at all times that less than the truth is a lie; that evasion, excuse-making, and exaggeration are all halfway houses towards what is false and ought to be avoided. Encourage them in any circumstances to be straightforward, and, whatever it may cost them, to speak the truth.

I press this subject on your attention not merely for the sake of your children's character in the world, though I might dwell much on this. I urge it rather for your own comfort and assistance in all your dealings with them. You will find it a mighty help, indeed, to be able always to trust their word. It will go far to prevent that habit of concealment, which so unhappily prevails sometimes among children. Openness and straight-forwardness depend much upon a parent's treatment of this matter in the days of our infancy.

CHAPTER 15

TRAIN THEM TO A HABIT OF
ALWAYS REDEEMING THE TIME

Idleness is the devil's best friend. It is the surest way to give him an opportunity of doing us harm. An idle mind is like an open door and, if Satan does not enter in himself by it, it is certain he will throw in something to raise bad thoughts in our souls.

No created being was ever meant to be idle. Service and work is the appointed portion of every creature of God. The angels in heaven work, they are the Lord's ministering servants, ever doing His will. Adam, in Paradise, had work. He was appointed to dress the garden of Eden and to keep it. The redeemed saints in glory will have work, "They rest not day and night singing praise and glory to Him who bought them." And man, weak, sinful man, must have something to do or else his soul will soon get into an unhealthy state. We must have our hands filled and our minds occupied with something or else our imaginations will soon ferment and breed mischief.

And what is true of us is true of our children, too. Alas,

indeed, for the man that has nothing to do! The Jews thought idleness a positive sin. It was a law of theirs that every man should bring up his son to some useful trade and they were right. They knew the heart of man better than some of us appear to do.

Idleness made Sodom what she was. "This was the iniquity of thy sister Sodom, pride, fullness of bread, and abundance of idleness was in her" (Ez 16:49). Idleness had much to do with David's awful sin with the wife of Uriah. I see in 2 Samuel 11 that Joab went out to war against Ammon, "but David tarried still at Jerusalem." Was not that idle? And then it was that he saw Bathsheba and the next step we read of is his tremendous and miserable fall.

Verily, I believe that idleness has led to more sin than almost any other habit that could be named. I suspect it is the mother of many a work of the flesh; the mother of adultery, fornication, drunkenness, and many other deeds of darkness that I have not time to name. Let your own conscience say whether I do not speak the truth. You were idle and at once the devil knocked at the door and came in.

And, indeed, I do not wonder; everything in the world around us seems to teach the same lesson. It is the still water, which becomes stagnant and impure; the running, moving streams are always clear. If you have steam machinery, you must work it or it soon gets out of order. If you have a horse, you must exercise him; he is never so well as when he has regular work. If you would have good bodily health yourself, you must take exercise. If you always sit still, your body is sure at length to complain. And just so is it with the soul. The active moving mind is a hard mark for the devil to shoot at. Try to be always full of useful employment and thus your enemy will find it difficult to get room to sow tares.

Reader, I ask you to set these things before the minds of your children. Teach them the value of time and try to make them learn the habit of using it well. It pains me to see children idling over what they have in hand, whatever it may be. I love to see them active and industrious, giving their whole heart to all they do; giving their whole heart to lessons, when they have to learn; giving their whole heart even to their amusements, when they go to play.

But if you love them well, let idleness be counted a sin in your family.

CHAPTER 16

TRAIN THEM WITH A CONSTANT FEAR OF OVER-INDULGENCE

This is the one point of all on which you have most need to be on your guard. It is natural to be tender and affectionate towards your own flesh and blood, and it is the excess of this very tenderness and affection that you have to fear. Take heed that it does not make you blind to your children's faults and deaf to all advice about them. Take heed lest it make you overlook bad conduct, rather than have the pain of inflicting punishment and correction.

I know well that punishment and correction are disagreeable things. Nothing is more unpleasant than giving pain to those we love and calling forth their tears. But so long as hearts are what hearts are, it is vain to suppose as a general rule that children can ever be brought up without correction.

Spoiling is a very expressive word, and sadly full of meaning. Now it is the shortest way to spoil children to let them have their own way, to allow them to do wrong, and not to punish them for it. Believe me, you must not do it, whatever pain it may cost you unless you wish to ruin your children's souls.

You cannot say that Scripture does not speak expressly on this subject: "He that spares his rod, hates his son; but he that loves him, chastens him betimes" (Prov 13:24). "Chasten thy son while there is hope, and let not thy soul spare for his crying" (Prov 19:18). "Foolishness is bound in the heart of a child: but the rod of correction shall drive it from him" (Prov 22:15). "Withhold not correction from the child, for if thou beat him with the rod he shall not die. Thou shall beat him with the rod, and deliver his soul from hell" (Prov 23:13,14). "The rod and reproof give wisdom: but a child left to himself brings his mother to shame." "Correct thy son, and he shall give thee rest, yea, he shall give delight to thy soul" (Prov 29:15,17).

How strong and forcible are these texts! How melancholy is the fact, that in many Christian families, they seem almost unknown! Their children need reproof, but it is hardly ever given; they need correction, but it is hardly ever employed. And yet this book of Proverbs is not obsolete and unfit for Christians. It is given by inspiration of God and profitable. It is given for our learning, even as the Epistles to the Romans and Ephesians. Surely the believer who brings up his children without attention to its counsel is making himself wise above that which is written and greatly errs.

Fathers and mothers, I tell you plainly, if you never punish your children when they are in fault, you are doing them a grievous wrong. I warn you, this is the rock on which the saints of God, in every age, have only too frequently made shipwreck. I would fain persuade you to be wise in time and keep clear of it. See it in Eli's case. His sons Hophni and Phinehas "made themselves vile, and he restrained them not." He gave them no more than a tame and lukewarm reproof when he ought to have rebuked them sharply. In one word, he honored his sons above God. And what was the end of these things? He lived to hear of the death of both his sons in battle, and his own grey hairs were brought down with sorrow to the grave (1 Samuel 2:22–29, 3:13).

See, too, the case of David. Who can read without pain the history of his children and their sins? Amnon's incest, Absalom's murder and proud rebellion, and Adonijah's scheming ambition. Truly these were grievous wounds for the man after God's own heart to receive from his own house. But was there no fault on his side? I fear there can be no doubt there was. I find a clue to it all in the account of Adonijah in 1 Kings 1:6: "His father had not displeased him at any time in saying, Why hast thou done so?" There was the foundation of all the mischief. David was an over-indulgent father, a father who let his children have their own way, and he reaped according as he had sown.

Parents, I beseech you, for your children's sake, beware of

over-indulgence. I call on you to remember, it is your first duty to consult their real interests, and not their fancies and likings; to train them, not to humor them to profit, not merely to please.

You must not give way to every wish and caprice of your child's mind, however much you may love him. You must not let him suppose his will is to be everything and that he has only to desire a thing and it will be done. Do not, I pray you, make your children idols, lest God should take them away and break your idol, just to convince you of your folly.

Learn to say "No" to your children. Show them that you are able to refuse whatever you think is not fit for them. Show them that you are ready to punish disobedience and that when you speak of punishment, you are not only ready to threaten, but also to perform. Do not threaten too much. Threatened folks and threatened faults, live long. Punish seldom, but really and in good earnest, frequent and slight punishment is a wretched system indeed.

Some parents and nurses have a way of saying, "Naughty child," to a boy or girl on every slight occasion, and often without good cause. It is a very foolish habit. Words of blame should never be used without real reason.

As to the best way of punishing a child, no general rule can be laid down. The characters of children are so exceedingly different that what would be a severe punishment to one child would be no punishment at all to another. I only beg to enter my decided protest against the modern notion that no child ought ever to be whipped. Doubtless some parents use bodily correction far too much and far too violently. But many others, I fear, use it far too little.

Beware of letting small faults pass unnoticed under the idea "it is a little one." There are no little things in training children; all are important. Little weeds need plucking up as much as any. Leave them alone and they will soon be great.

Reader, if there be any point which deserves your attention, believe me, it is this one. It is one that will give you trouble, I know. But if you do not take trouble with your children when they are young, they will give you trouble when they are old. Choose which you prefer.

CHAPTER 17

TRAIN THEM REMEMBERING CONTINUALLY HOW GOD TRAINS HIS CHILDREN.

The Bible tells us that God has an elect people, a family in this world. All poor sinners who have been convinced of sin and fled to Jesus for peace, make up that family. All of us who really believe on Christ for salvation are its members.

Now God the Father is ever training the members of this family for their everlasting abode with Him in heaven. He acts as a husbandman pruning his vines, that they may bear more fruit. He knows the character of each of us—our besetting sins, our weaknesses, our peculiar infirmities, and our special wants. He knows our works and where we dwell, who are our companions in life, what are our trials, what our temptations, and what are our privileges. He knows all these things and is ever ordering all for our good. He allots to each of us, in His providence, the very things we need, in order to bear the most fruit; as much of sunshine as we can stand, as much of rain, as much of bitter things as we can bear, and as much of sweet. Reader, if you would train your children wisely, mark well how

God the Father trains His. He doeth all things well; the plan that He adopts must be right.

See, then, how many things there are which God withholds from His children. Few could be found, I suspect, among them who have not had desires that He has never been pleased to fulfill. There has often been some one thing they wanted to attain, and, yet, there has always been some barrier to prevent attainment. It has been just as if God was placing it above our reach, and saying, "This is not good for you; this must not be." Moses desired exceedingly to cross over Jordan and see the goodly land of promise; but you will remember his desire was never granted.

See, too, how often God leads His people by ways which seem dark and mysterious to our eyes. We cannot see the meaning of all His dealings with us; we cannot see the reasonableness of the path in which our feet are treading. Sometimes so many trials have assailed us, so many difficulties encompassed us, that we have not been able to discover the needs-be of it all. It has been just as if our Father was taking us by the hand into a dark place and saying, "Ask no questions, but follow Me." There was a direct road from Egypt to Canaan, yet Israel was not led into it, but round, through the wilderness. And this seemed hard at the time. "The soul of the people," we are told, "was much discouraged because of the way" (Ex 13:17; Num 21:4).

See, also, how often God chastens His people with trial and affliction. He sends them crosses and disappointments; He lays them low with sickness; He strips them of property and friends; He changes them from one position to another; He visits them with things most hard to flesh and blood; and some of us have well-nigh fainted under the burdens laid upon us. We have felt pressed beyond strength, and have been almost ready to murmur at the hand that chastened us. Paul the Apostle had a thorn in the flesh appointed him, some bitter bodily trial, no doubt, though we know not exactly what it was. But this we know, he besought the Lord thrice that it might be removed; yet it was not taken away (2 Cor 12:8–9).

Now, reader, notwithstanding all these things, did you ever hear of a single child of God who thought his Father did not treat him wisely? No, I am sure you never did. God's children would always tell you, in the long run, it was a blessed thing they did not have their own way and that God had done far better for them than they could have done for themselves. Yes! And they could tell you, too, that God's dealings had provided more happiness for them than they ever would have obtained themselves and that His way, however dark at times, was the way of pleasantness and the path of peace.

I ask you to lay to heart the lesson, which God's dealings with His people, is meant to teach you. Fear not to withhold from your child anything you think will do him harm, whatever his own wishes may be. This is God's plan.

Hesitate not to lay on him commands of which he may not at present see the wisdom and to guide him in ways that may not now seem reasonable to his mind. This is God's plan.

Shrink not from chastising and correcting him whenever you see his soul's health requires it, however painful it may be to your feelings; and remember medicines for the mind must not be rejected because they are bitter. This is God's plan.

And be not afraid, above all, that such a plan of training will make your child unhappy. I warn you against this delusion. Depend on it. There is no surer road to unhappiness than always having our own way. To have our wills checked and denied is a blessed thing for us; it makes us value enjoyments when they come. To be indulged perpetually is the way to be made selfish; and selfish people and spoiled children, believe me, are seldom happy.

Reader, be not wiser than God; train your children as He trains His.

CHAPTER 18

TRAIN THEM REMEMBERING CONTINUALLY THE INFLUENCE OF YOUR OWN EXAMPLE

Instruction, advice, and commands will profit little, unless they are backed up by the pattern of your own life. Your children will never believe you are in earnest and really wish them to obey you, so long as your actions contradict your counsel. Archbishop Tillotson made a wise remark when he said, "To give children good instruction and a bad example is but beckoning to them with the head to show them the way to heaven, while we take them by the hand and lead them in the way to hell."

We little know the force and power of example. No one of us can live to himself in this world; we are always influencing those around us, in one way or another, either for good or for evil, either for God or for sin. They see our ways, they mark our conduct, they observe our behavior, and what they see us practice, they may fairly suppose we think right. And never, I believe, does example tell so powerfully as it does in the case of parents and children.

Fathers and mothers, do not forget that children learn more by the eye than they do by the ear. No school will make such deep marks on character as home. The best of schoolmasters will not imprint on their minds as much as they will pick up at your fireside. Imitation is a far stronger principle with children than memory. What they see has a much stronger effect on their minds than what they are told.

Take care, then, what you do before a child. It is a true proverb, "Who sins before a child, sins double." Strive rather to be a living epistle of Christ, such as your families can read and that plainly too. Be an example of reverence for the Word of God, reverence in prayer, reverence for means of grace, reverence for the Lord's Day. Be an example in words, in temper, in diligence, in temperance, in faith, in charity, in kindness, in humility. Think not your children will practice what they do not see you do. You are their model picture and they will copy what you are. Your reasoning and your lecturing, your wise commands and your good advice; all this they may not understand, but they can understand your life.

Children are very quick observers; very quick in seeing through some kinds of hypocrisy, very quick in finding out what you really think and feel, very quick in adopting all your ways and opinions. You will often find as the father is, so is the son.

Remember the word that the conqueror Caesar always used

to his soldiers in a battle. He did not say, "Go forward," but "Come." So it must be with you in training your children. They will seldom learn habits that they see you despise or walk in paths in which you do not walk yourself. He that preaches to his children what he does not practice is working a work that never goes forward. It is like the fabled web of Penelope of old, who wove all-day and unwove all night. Even so, the parent who tries to train without setting a good example is building with one hand and pulling down with the other.

CHAPTER 19

TRAIN THEM REMEMBERING CONTINUALLY THE POWER OF SIN

I name this shortly in order to guard you against unscriptural expectations. You must not expect to find your children's minds a sheet of pure white paper and to have no trouble if you only use right means. I warn you plainly you will find no such thing. It is painful to see how much corruption and evil there is in a young child's heart and how soon it begins to bear fruit. Violent tempers, self-will, pride, envy, sullenness, passion, idleness, selfishness, deceit, cunning, falsehood, hypocrisy, a terrible aptness to learn what is bad, a painful slowness to learn what is good, a readiness to pretend anything in order to gain their own ends, all these things, or some of them, you must be prepared to see, even in your own flesh and blood. In little ways they will creep out at a very early age. It is almost startling to observe how naturally they seem to spring up. Children require no schooling to learn to sin.

But you must not be discouraged and cast down by what you see. You must not think it a strange and unusual thing that little hearts can be so full of sin. It is the only portion which our father Adam left us. It is that fallen nature with which we come into the world. It is that inheritance which belongs to us all. Let it rather make you more diligent in using every means, which seem most likely, by God's blessing, to counteract the mischief. Let it make you more and more careful, so far as in you lies, to keep your children out of the way of temptation.

Never listen to those who tell you your children are good, well brought up, and can be trusted. Think rather that their hearts are always inflammable as tinder. At their very best, they only want a spark to set their corruptions alight. Parents are seldom too cautious. Remember the natural depravity of your children and take care.

TRAIN THEM REMEMBERING CONTINUALLY THE PROMISES OF SCRIPTURE

I name this also, shortly, in order to guard you against discouragement.

You have a plain promise on your side, "Train up your child in the way he should go, and when he is old he shall not depart from it" (Prov 22:6). Think what it is to have a promise like this. Promises were the only lamp of hope that cheered the hearts of the patriarchs before the Bible was written. Enoch, Noah, Abraham, Isaac, Jacob, Joseph, all lived on a few promises and prospered in their souls. Promises are the cordials that in every age have supported and strengthened the believer. He that has got a plain text upon his side need never be cast down. Fathers and mothers, when your hearts are failing and ready to halt, look at the word of this text and take comfort.

Think who it is that promises. It is not the word of a man who may lie or repent; it is the word of the King of kings who never changes. Hath He said a thing and shall He not do it? Or hath He spoken and shall He not make it good? Neither is anything too hard for Him to perform. The things that are impossible with men are possible with God. Reader, if we get not the benefit of the promise we are dwelling upon, the fault is not in Him, but in ourselves.

Think, too, what the promise contains, before you refuse to take comfort from it. It speaks of a certain time when good training shall especially bear fruit, "when a child is old." Surely there is comfort in this. You may not see with your own eyes the result of careful training, but you know not what blessed fruits may not spring from it, long after you are dead and gone. It is not God's way to give everything at once. "Afterwards" is the time when He often chooses to work, both in the things of nature and in the things of grace. "Afterward" is the season when affliction bears the peaceable fruit of righteousness (Heb 12:11). "Afterward" was the time when the son who refused to work in his father's vineyard repented and went (Matt 21:29). And "afterward" is the time to which parents must look forward, if they see not success at once. You must sow in hope and plant in hope.

"Cast thy bread upon the waters," says the Spirit, "for thou shall find it after many days" (Eccl 11:1). Many children, I doubt not, shall rise up in the day of judgment, and bless their parents for good training, who never gave any signs of having profited by it during their parents' lives. Go forward then in faith and be sure that your labor shall not be altogether thrown away. Three times did Elijah stretch himself upon the widow's child before it revived. Take example from him and persevere.

CHAPTER 21

TRAIN THEM, LASTLY, WITH CONTINUAL PRAYER FOR A BLESSING ON ALL YOU DO

Without the blessing of the Lord, your best endeavors will do no good. He has the hearts of all men in His hands and, except He touch the hearts of your children by His Spirit, you will weary yourself to no purpose. Water, therefore, the seed you sow on their minds with unceasing prayer. The Lord is far more willing to hear than we to pray; far more ready to give blessings than we to ask them; but He loves to be entreated for them. And I set this matter of prayer before you as the top-stone and seal of all you do. I suspect the child of many prayers is seldom cast away.

Look upon your children as Jacob did on his. He tells Esau they are "the children which God hath graciously given thy servant" (Gen 33: 5). Look on them as Joseph did on his. He told his father, "They are the sons whom God hath given me" (Gen 48:9). Count them with the Psalmist to be "an heritage and reward from the Lord" (Ps 127:3). And then ask the Lord, with a holy boldness, to be gracious and merciful to His own gifts. Mark how Abraham intercedes for Ishmael because he loved him: "Oh that Ishmael might live before thee" (Gen 17:18). See how Manoah speaks to the angel about Samson: "How shall we order the child, and how shall we do unto him?" (Judg 13:12). Observe how tenderly Job cared for his children's souls: "He offered burnt-offerings according to the number of them all, for he said, 'It may be my sons have sinned, and cursed God in their hearts.' Thus did Job continually" (Job 1:5). Parents, if you love your children, go and do likewise. You cannot name their names before the mercy seat too often.

And now, reader, in conclusion, let me once more press upon you the necessity and importance of using every single means in your power, if you would train children for heaven.

I know well that God is a sovereign God and doeth all things according to the counsel of His own will. I know that Rehoboam was the son of Solomon, Manasseh the son of Hezekiah, and that you do not always see godly parents having a godly seed. But I know also that God is a God who works by means, and sure am I, if you make light of such means as I have mentioned, your children are not likely to turn out well. Fathers and mothers, you may take your children to be baptized and have them enrolled in the ranks of Christ's Church; you may get godly sponsors to answer for them and help you by their prayers; you may send them to the best of schools and give them Bibles, Prayer Books, and fill them with head knowledge; but, if all this time there is no regular training at home, I tell you plainly, I fear it will go hard in the end with your children's souls. Home is the place where habits are formed. Home is the place where the foundations of character are laid. Home gives the bias to our tastes, likings, and opinions. See then, I pray you, that there be careful training at home. Happy indeed is the man who can say, as Bolton did upon his dying bed to his children, "I do believe not one of you will dare to meet me before the tribunal of Christ in an unregenerate state."

Fathers and mothers, I charge you solemnly before God and the Lord Jesus Christ, take every pain to train your children in the way they should go. I charge you not merely for the sake of your children's souls; I charge you for the sake of your own future comfort and peace. Truly it is your interest so to do. Truly your own happiness in great measure depends on it. Children have ever been the bow from which the sharpest arrows have pierced man's heart. Children have mixed the bitterest cups that man has ever had to drink. Children have caused the saddest tears that man has ever had to shed. Adam could tell you so. Jacob could tell you so. David could tell you so. There are no sorrows on earth like those that children have brought upon their parents. Oh! Take heed, lest your own neglect should lay up misery for you in your old age. Take heed, lest you weep under the ill treatment of a thankless child in the days when your eye is dim and your natural force abated.

If ever you wish your children to be the restorers of your

life and the nourishers of your old age; if you would have them blessings and not curses, joys and not sorrows, Judahs and not Reubens, Ruths and not Orpahs; if you would not, like Noah, be ashamed of their deeds, and, like Rebekah, be made weary of your life by them: if this be your wish, remember my advice betimes, train them while young in the right way. And as for me, I will conclude by putting up my prayer to God for all who read this paper, that you may all be taught of God to feel the value of your own souls. This is one reason why baptism is too often a mere form and Christian training despised and disregarded. Too often parents feel not for themselves, and so they feel not for their children. They do not realize the tremendous difference between a state of nature and a state of grace, and, therefore, they are content to let them alone.

Now the Lord teach you all that sin is that abominable thing which God hates. Then, I know you will mourn over the sins of your children and strive to pluck them out as brands from the fire.

The Lord teach you all how precious Christ is and what a mighty and complete work He hath done for our salvation. Then, I feel confident you will use every means to bring your children to Jesus that they may live through Him.

The Lord teach you all your need of the Holy Spirit, to renew, sanctify, and quicken your souls. Then, I feel sure you will urge your children to pray for Him without ceasing and never rest till He has come down into their hearts with power and made them new creatures.

The Lord grant this and then I have a good hope that you will indeed train up your children well. Train them well for this life and train them well for the life to come; train them well for earth and train them well for heaven; train them for God, for Christ, and for eternity.

CONCLUSION

The world has never known even one perfect parent. In the history of humanity, there were only ever two individuals with the potential for becoming perfect parents. Not until after Adam and Eve had rejected God and carried out the evil desires of their heart do we read that they bore children (Genesis 4). The only two individuals who could have been perfect parents were not perfect by the time they became parents. As a result, all of their descendants born into this world possess a fallen nature bent to sin and self. Therefore, no parent has ever been entrusted as a perfect human being to carry forward God's mission to be fruitful and multiply image-bearing worshippers who live in a personal relationship with Him.

If God, then, were only ever going to use perfect people to accomplish His mission, He would have no one to use except Himself. Specifically, if God were only going to use perfect parents to make disciples of their children, there would be no parents available to do the work and no children would ever be made disciples of Jesus Christ. We dare not celebrate being fallen or use it as an excuse for our ongoing rejection and rebellion against God. Yet, we can celebrate that God can and does use imperfect people to accomplish His perfect will and mission. We are encouraged by the fact God has and continues to use imperfect parents with all their frailty to fulfill the task of making disciples of their children through all generations.[1] Wayne Rice challenges, "Your children don't require parents who have it all together. Obviously, you want to practice what you preach, but none of us do that perfectly. If you want to lead your children to walk with God, the best thing you can do is do all you can to stay on the road yourself and walk alongside of them."[2] In other words, God uses imperfect people as instruments to bring about change in others through His mission of making disciples, even when those He uses are still in need of being changed themselves.[3]

As you either embark on the journey of parenthood, continue to walk its path, or enter the new season of being a grandparent, let the words of God dwell in you deeply and abundantly. God has called you to the spiritual task of spiritual leadership of your children and grandchildren. Even though you sin and fall short, even when you still have areas where you

---

[1] J. I. Packer and Carolyn Nystrom, *Never Beyond Hope: How God Touches & Uses Imperfect People* (Downers Grove, IL: InterVarsity Press, 2000), 24; Warren Wiersbe, *The Wiersbe Bible Commentary: Old Testament* (Colorado Springs, CO: David C. Cook, 2007), 144.

[2] Wayne Rice, *Generation to Generation* (Cincinnati, OH: Standard, 2010), 32.

[3] See Paul Tripp, *Instruments in the Redeemer's Hands* (Phillipsburg, NJ: P&R Publishing, 2002).

need to be transformed by the power of Jesus Christ, God intends to use you in passing on faith to the next generation through your children.

God has given you all that you need to lead and influence your children to surrender their lives to follow Jesus Christ in a personal relationship of worship and obedience. The task is not clean or easy, but eternally worth it! We can trust that, in spite of the fact we are imperfect people and incapable of fulfilling His mission on our own. God is able to work in and through us by the power of Christ. He is able to accomplish more than we can ask (Eph 3:20). Believe Him for this and follow Him in this!

Made in the USA
Middletown, DE
17 May 2022

65883003R00099